Train To Pakistan

By Khushwant Singh

GREENWOOD PRESS, PUBLISHERS
WESTPORT, CONNECTICUT

Library of Congress Cataloging in Publication Data

Singh, Khushwant.
   Train to Pakistan.

   Reprint of the Black cat ed. published by Grove Press,
New York.
   I.   Title.
PZ4.S6182Tr4   [PR9480.9.S5]   823   75-15688
ISBN 0-8371-8226-3

Originally published in 1956 by Grove Press, Inc., New York

Reprinted with the permission of Grove Press, Inc.

Reprinted in 1975 by Greenwood Press,
a division of Williamhouse-Regency Inc.

Library of Congress Catalog Card Number 75-15688

ISBN 0-8371-8226-3

Printed in the United States of America

For My Daughter

MALA

DACOITY

THE summer of 1947 was not like other Indian summers. Even the weather had a different feel in India that year. It was hotter than usual, and drier and dustier. And the summer was longer. No one could remember when the monsoon had been so late. For weeks, the sparse clouds cast only shadows. There was no rain. People began to say that God was punishing them for their sins.

Some of them had good reason to feel that they had sinned. The summer before, communal riots, precipitated by reports of the proposed division of the country into a Hindu India and a Muslim Pakistan, had broken out in Calcutta, and within a few months the death roll had mounted to several thousand. Muslims said the Hindus had planned and started the killing. According to the Hindus, the Muslims were to blame. The fact is, both sides killed. Both shot and stabbed and speared and clubbed. Both tortured. Both raped. From Calcutta, the riots spread north and east and west: to Noakhali in East Bengal, where Muslims massacred Hindus; to Bihar, where Hindus massacred Muslims. Mullahs roamed the Punjab and the Frontier Province with boxes of human skulls said to be those of Muslims killed in Bihar. Hundreds of thousands of Hindus and Sikhs who had lived for centuries on the Northwest Frontier abandoned their homes and fled toward the protection of the predominantly Sikh and Hindu communities in the east. They traveled on foot, in bullock carts, crammed into lorries, clinging to the sides and roofs of trains. Along the way—at fords, at crossroads, at railroad stations—they collided with panicky swarms of Muslims fleeing to safety in the west. The riots had become a rout. By the summer of 1947, when the creation of the new state of Pakistan was formally announced, ten million people—Muslims and Hindus and Sikhs—were in flight. By the time the monsoon broke, almost a million of them were dead, and all of northern India was in arms, in terror, or in hiding. The only remaining oases of peace were a scatter of little villages lost in the remote reaches of the frontier. One of these villages was Mano Majra.

Mano Majra is a tiny place. It has only three brick buildings, one of which is the home of the moneylender Lala Ram Lal. The other two are the Sikh temple and the mosque. The three brick buildings enclose a triangular common with a large peepul tree in the middle. The rest of the village is a cluster of flat-roofed mud huts and low-walled courtyards, which front on narrow lanes that radiate from the center. Soon the lanes dwindle into footpaths and get lost in the surrounding fields. At the western end of the village there is a pond ringed round by keekar trees. There are only about seventy families in Mano Majra, and Lala Ram Lal's is the only Hindu family. The others are Sikhs or Muslims, about equal in number. The Sikhs own all the land around the village; the Muslims are tenants and share the tilling with the owners. There are a few families of sweepers whose religion is uncertain. The Muslims claim them as their own, yet when American missionaries visit Mano Majra the sweepers wear khaki sola topees and join their womenfolk in singing hymns to the accompaniment of a harmonium. Sometimes they visit the Sikh temple, too. But there is one object that all Mano Majrans—even Lala Ram Lal—venerate. This is a three-foot slab of sandstone that stands upright under a keekar tree beside the pond. It is the local deity, the *deo* to which all the villagers—Hindu, Sikh, Muslim or pseudo-Christian—repair secretly whenever they are in special need of blessing.

Although Mano Majra is said to be on the banks of the Sutlej River, it is actually half a mile away from it. In India villages cannot afford to be too close to the banks of rivers. Rivers change their moods with the seasons and alter their courses

2

without warning. The Sutlej is the largest river in the Punjab. After the monsoon its waters rise and spread across its vast sandy bed, lapping high up the mud embankments on either side. It becomes an expanse of muddy turbulence more than a mile in breadth. When the flood subsides, the river breaks up into a thousand shallow streams that wind sluggishly between little marshy islands. About a mile north of Mano Majra the Sutlej is spanned by a railroad bridge. It is a magnificent bridge —its eighteen enormous spans sweep like waves from one pier to another, and at each end of it there is a stone embankment to buttress the railway line. On the eastern end the embankment extends all the way to the village railroad station.

Mano Majra has always been known for its railway station. Since the bridge has only one track, the station has several sidings where less important trains can wait, to make way for the more important.

A small colony of shopkeepers and hawkers has grown up around the station to supply travelers with food, betel leaves, cigarettes, tea, biscuits and sweetmeats. This gives the station an appearance of constant activity and its staff a somewhat exaggerated sense of importance. Actually the stationmaster himself sells tickets through the pigeonhole in his office, collects them at the exit beside the door, and sends and receives messages over the telegraph ticker on his table. When there are people to notice him, he comes out on the platform and waves a green flag for trains which do not stop. His only assistant manipulates the levers in the glass cabin on the platform which control the signals on either side, and helps shunting engines by changing hand points on the tracks to get them onto the sidings. In the evenings, he lights the long line of lamps on the platform. He takes heavy aluminum lamps to the signals and sticks them in the clamps behind the red and green glass. In the mornings, he brings them back and puts out the lights on the platform.

Not many trains stop at Mano Majra. Express trains do not

stop at all. Of the many slow passenger trains, only two, one from Delhi to Lahore in the mornings and the other from Lahore to Delhi in the evenings, are scheduled to stop for a few minutes. The others stop only when they are held up. The only regular customers are the goods trains. Although Mano Majra seldom has any goods to send or receive, its station sidings are usually occupied by long rows of wagons. Each passing goods train spends hours shedding wagons and collecting others. After dark, when the countryside is steeped in silence, the whistling and puffing of engines, the banging of buffers, and the clanking of iron couplings can be heard all through the night.

All this has made Mano Majra very conscious of trains. Before daybreak, the mail train rushes through on its way to Lahore, and as it approaches the bridge, the driver invariably blows two long blasts of the whistle. In an instant, all Mano Majra comes awake. Crows begin to caw in the keekar trees. Bats fly back in long silent relays and begin to quarrel for their perches in the peepul. The mullah at the mosque knows that it is time for the morning prayer. He has a quick wash, stands facing west toward Mecca and with his fingers in his ears cries in long sonorous notes, "Allah-ho-Akbar." The priest at the Sikh temple lies in bed till the mullah has called. Then he too gets up, draws a bucket of water from the well in the temple courtyard, pours it over himself, and intones his prayer in monotonous singsong to the sound of splashing water.

By the time the 10:30 morning passenger train from Delhi comes in, life in Mano Majra has settled down to its dull daily routine. Men are in the fields. Women are busy with their daily chores. Children are out grazing cattle by the river. Persian wheels squeak and groan as bullocks go round and round, prodded on by curses and the jabs of goads in their hindquarters. Sparrows fly about the roofs, trailing straw in their beaks. Pye-dogs seek the shade of the long mud walls. Bats settle their arguments, fold their wings, and suspend themselves in sleep.

As the midday express goes by, Mano Majra stops to rest.

Men and children come home for dinner and the siesta hour. When they have eaten, the men gather in the shade of the peepul tree and sit on the wooden platforms and talk and doze. Boys ride their buffaloes into the pond, jump off their backs, and splash about in the muddy water. Girls play under the trees. Women rub clarified butter into each other's hair, pick lice from their children's heads, and discuss births, marriages and deaths.

When the evening passenger from Lahore comes in, everyone gets to work again. The cattle are rounded up and driven back home to be milked and locked in for the night. The women cook the evening meal. Then the families foregather on their rooftops where most of them sleep during the summer. Sitting on their charpoys, they eat their supper of vegetables and chapatties and sip hot creamy milk out of large copper tumblers and idle away the time until the signal for sleep. When the goods train steams in, they say to each other, "There is the goods train." It is like saying goodnight. The mullah again calls the faithful to prayer by shouting at the top of his voice, "God is great." The faithful nod their amens from their rooftops. The Sikh priest murmurs the evening prayer to a semicircle of drowsy old men and women. Crows caw softly from the keekar trees. Little bats go flitting about in the dusk and large ones soar with slow graceful sweeps. The goods train takes a long time at the station, with the engine running up and down the sidings exchanging wagons. By the time it leaves, the children are asleep. The older people wait for its rumble over the bridge to lull them to slumber. Then life in Mano Majra is stilled, save for the dogs barking at the trains that pass in the night.

It had always been so, until the summer of 1947.

One heavy night in August of that year, five men emerged from a keekar grove not far from Mano Majra, and moved silently toward the river. They were dacoits, or professional robbers, and all but one of them were armed. Two of the armed men carried spears. The others had carbines slung over their shoulders. The fifth man carried a chromium-plated electric torch. When they came to the embankment, he flicked the torch alight. Then he grunted and snapped it off.

"We will wait here," he said.

He dropped down on the sand. The others crouched around him, leaning on their weapons. The man with the torch looked at one of the spearmen.

"You have the bangles for Jugga?"

"Yes. A dozen of red and blue glass. They would please any village wench."

"They will not please Jugga," one of the gunmen said.

The leader laughed. He tossed the torch in the air and caught it. He laughed again and raised the torch to his mouth and touched the switch. His cheeks glowed pink from the light inside.

"Jugga could give the bangles to that weaver's daughter of his," the other spearman said. "They would look well with those large gazelle eyes and the little mango breasts. What is her name?"

The leader turned off the torch and took it from his mouth. "Nooran," he said.

"Aho," the spearman said. "Nooran. Did you see her at the spring fair? Did you see that tight shirt showing off her breasts and the bells tinkling in her plaits and the swish-swish of silk? Hai!"

"Hai!" the spearman with the bangles cried. "Hai! Hai!"

"She must give Jugga a good time," said the gunman who had not yet spoken. "During the day, she looks so innocent you would think she had not shed her milk teeth." He sighed. "But at night, she puts black antimony in her eyes."

"Antimony is good for the eyes," one of the others said. "It is cooling."

"It is good for other people's eyes as well," the gunman said.

"And cooling to their passions, too."

"Jugga?" the leader said.

The others laughed. One of them suddenly sat erect.

"Listen!" he said. "There is the goods train."

The others stopped laughing. They all listened in silence to the approaching train. It came to a halt with a rumble, and the wagons groaned and creaked. After a time, the engine could be heard moving up and down, releasing wagons. There were loud explosions as the released wagons collided with the ones on the sidings. The engine chuffed back to the train.

"It is time to call on Ram Lal," the leader said, and got to his feet.

His companions rose and brushed the sand off their clothes. They formed a line with their hands joined in prayer. One of the gunmen stepped in front and began to mumble. When he stopped, they all went down on their knees and rubbed their foreheads on the ground. Then they stood up and drew the loose ends of their turbans across their faces. Only their eyes were uncovered. The engine gave two long whistle blasts, and the train moved off toward the bridge.

"Now," the leader said.

The others followed him up the embankment and across the fields. By the time the train had reached the bridge, the men had skirted the pond and were walking up a lane that led to the center of the village. They came to the house of Lala Ram Lal. The leader nodded to one of the gunmen. He stepped forward and began to pound on the door with the butt of his gun.

"Oi!" he shouted. "Lala!"

There was no reply. Village dogs gathered round the visitors and began to bark. One of the men hit a dog with the flat side of his spear blade. Another fired his gun into the air. The dogs ran away whimpering and started to bark louder from a safer distance.

The men began to hammer at the door with their weapons. One struck it with his spear which went through to the other side.

"Open, you son of fornication, or we will kill the lot of you," he shouted.

A woman's voice answered. "Who is it who calls at this hour? Lalaji has gone to the city."

"Open and we will tell you who we are or we will smash the door," the leader said.

"I tell you Lalaji is not in. He has taken the keys with him. We have nothing in the house."

The men put their shoulders to the door, pressed, pulled back and butted into it like battering-rams. The wooden bolt on the other side cracked and the doors flew open. One of the men with a gun waited at the door; the other four went in. In one corner of the room two women sat crouching. A boy of seven with large black eyes clung to the older of the two.

"In the name of God, take what we have, all our jewelry, everything," implored the older woman. She held out a handful of gold and silver bracelets, anklets and earrings.

One of the men snatched them from her hands.

"Where is the Lala?"

"I swear by the Guru he is out. You have taken all we have. Lalaji has nothing more to give."

In the courtyard four beds were laid out in a row.

The man with the carbine tore the little boy from his grandmother's lap and held the muzzle of the gun to the child's face. The women fell at his feet imploring.

"Do not kill, brother. In the name of the Guru—don't."

The gunman kicked the women away.

"Where is your father?"

The boy shook with fear and stuttered, "Upstairs."

The gunman thrust the boy back into the woman's lap, and the men went out into the courtyard and climbed the staircase. There was only one room on the roof. Without pausing they put their shoulders to the door and pushed it in, tearing it off its hinges. The room was cluttered with steel trunks piled one on top of the other. There were two charpoys with several quilts rolled up on them. The white beam of the torch searched the room and caught the moneylender crouching under one of the charpoys.

"In the name of the Guru, the Lalaji is out," one of the men said, mimicking the woman's voice. He dragged Ram Lal out by his legs.

The leader slapped the moneylender with the back of his hand. "Is this the way you treat your guests? We come and you hide under a charpoy."

Ram Lal covered his face with his arms and began to whimper.

"Where are the keys of the safe?" asked the leader, kicking him on the behind.

"You can take all—jewelry, cash, account books. Don't kill anyone," implored the moneylender, grasping the leader's feet with both his hands.

"Where are the keys of your safe?" repeated the leader. He knocked the moneylender sprawling on the floor. Ram Lal sat up, shaking with fear.

He produced a wad of notes from his pocket. "Take these," he said, distributing the money to the five men. "It is all I have in the house. All is yours."

"Where are the keys of your safe?"

"There is nothing left in the safe; only my account books. I have given you all I have. All I have is yours. In the name of the Guru, let me be." Ram Lal clasped the leader's legs above the knees and began to sob. "In the name of the Guru! In the name of the Guru!"

One of the men tore the moneylender away from the leader and hit him full in the face with the butt of his gun.

"Hai!" yelled Ram Lal at the top of his voice, and spat out blood.

The women in the courtyard heard the cry and started shrieking, "Dakoo! dakoo!"

The dogs barked all round. But not a villager stirred from his house.

On the roof of his house, the moneylender was beaten with butts of guns and spear handles and kicked and punched. He sat on his haunches, crying and spitting blood. Two of his teeth were smashed. But he would not hand over the keys of his safe. In sheer exasperation, one of the men lunged at the crouching figure with his spear. Ram Lal uttered a loud yell and collapsed on the floor with blood spurting from his belly. The men came out. One of them fired two shots in the air. Women stopped wailing. Dogs stopped barking. The village was silenced.

The dacoits jumped off the roof to the lane below. They yelled defiance to the world as they went out towards the river.

"Come!" they yelled. "Come out, if you have the courage! Come out, if you want your mother and sisters raped! Come out, brave men!"

No one answered them. There was not a sound in Mano Majra. The men continued along the lane, shouting and laughing, until they came to a small hut on the edge of the village. The leader halted and motioned to one of the spearmen.

"This is the house of the great Jugga," he said. "Do not forget our gift. Give him his bangles."

The spearman dug a package from his clothes and tossed it over the wall. There was a muffled sound of breaking glass in the courtyard.

"O Juggia," he called in a falsetto voice, "Juggia!" He winked at his companions. "Wear these bangles, Juggia. Wear these bangles and put henna on your palms."

"Or give them to the weaver's daughter," one of the gunmen yelled.

"Hai," the others shouted They smacked their lips, making the sound of long, lecherous kisses. "Hai! Hai!"

They moved on down the lane, still laughing and blowing

kisses, toward the river. Juggut Singh did not answer them. He didn't hear them. He was not at home.

Juggut Singh had been gone from his home about an hour. He had only left when the sound of the night goods train told him that it would now be safe to go. For him, as for the dacoits, the arrival of the train that night was a signal. At the first distant rumble, he slipped quietly off his charpoy and picked up his turban and wrapped it round his head. Then he tiptoed across the courtyard to the haystack and fished out a spear. He tiptoed back to his bed, picked up his shoes, and crept toward the door.

"Where are you going?"

Juggut Singh stopped. It was his mother.

"To the fields," he said. "Last night wild pigs did a lot of damage."

"Pigs!" his mother said. "Don't try to be clever. Have you forgotten already that you are on probation—that it is forbidden for you to leave the village after sunset? And with a spear! Enemies will see you. They will report you. They will send you back to jail." Her voice rose to a wail. "Then who will look after the crops and the cattle?"

"I will be back soon," Juggut Singh said. "There is nothing to worry about. Everyone in the village is asleep."

"No," his mother said. She wailed again.

"Shut up," he said. "It is you who will wake the neighbors. Be quiet and there will be no trouble."

"Go! Go wherever you want to go. If you want to jump in a well, jump. If you want to hang like your father, go and hang. It is my lot to weep. My kismet," she added, slapping her forehead, "it is all written there."

Juggut Singh opened the door and looked on both sides. There was no one about. He walked along the walls till he got to the end of the lane near the pond. He could see the gray forms of a couple of adjutant storks slowly pacing up and down in the mud looking for frogs. They paused in their search. Juggut Singh stood still against the wall till the storks were reassured, then went off the footpath across the fields toward the river. He crossed the dry sand bed till he got to the stream. He stuck his spear in the ground with the blade pointing upward, then stretched out on the sand. He lay on his back and gazed at the stars. A meteor shot across the Milky Way, trailing a silver path down the blue-black sky. Suddenly a hand was on his eyes.

"Guess who?"

Juggut Singh stretched out his hands over his head and behind him, groping; the girl dodged them. Juggut Singh started with the hand on his eyes and felt his way up from the arm to the shoulder and then on to the face. He caressed her cheeks, eyes and nose that his hands knew so well. He tried to play with her lips to induce them to kiss his fingers. The girl opened her mouth and bit him fiercely. Juggut Singh jerked his hand away. With a quick movement he caught the girl's head in both his hands and brought her face over to his. Then he slipped his arms under her waist and hoisted her into the air above him with her arms and legs kicking about like a crab. He turned her about till his arms ached. He brought her down flat upon him limb to limb.

The girl slapped him on the face.

"You put your hands on the person of a strange woman. Have you no mother or sister in your home? Have you no shame? No wonder the police have got you on their register as a bad character. I will also tell the Inspector Sahib that you are a budmash."

"I am only budmash with you, Nooro. We should both be locked up in the same cell."

"You have learned to talk too much. I will have to look for another man."

Juggut Singh crossed his arms behind the girl's back and crushed her till she could not talk or breathe. Every time she started to speak he tightened his arms round her and her words got stuck in her throat. She gave up and put her exhausted face against his. He laid her beside him with her head nestling in the hollow of his left arm. With his right hand he stroked her hair and face.

The goods train engine whistled twice and with a lot of groaning and creaking began to puff its way toward the bridge. The storks flew up from the pond with shrill cries of "kraak, kraak" and came toward the river. From the river they flew back to the pond, calling alternately long after the train had gone over the bridge and its puff-puffs had died into silence.

Juggut Singh's caresses became lustful. His hand strayed from the girl's face to her breasts and her waist. She caught it and put it back on her face. His breathing became slow and sensuous. His hand wandered again and brushed against her breasts as if by mistake. The girl slapped it and put it away. Juggut Singh stretched his left arm that lay under the girl's head and caught her reproving hand. Her other arm was already under him. She was defenseless.

"No! No! No! Let go my hand! No! I will never speak to you again." She shook her head violently from side to side, trying to avoid his hungry mouth.

Juggut Singh slipped his hand inside her shirt and felt the contours of her unguarded breasts. They became taut. The nipples became hard and leathery. His rough hands gently moved up and down from her breasts to her navel. The skin on her belly came up in goose flesh.

The girl continued to wriggle and protest.

"No! No! No! Please. May Allah's curse fall on you. Let go my hand. I will never meet you again if you behave like this."

Juggut Singh's searching hand found one end of the cord of her trousers. He pulled it with a jerk.

"No," cried the girl hoarsely.

A shot rang through the night. The storks flew up from the pond calling to each other. Crows started cawing in the keekar

13

trees. Juggut Singh paused and looked up into the darkness towards the village. The girl quietly extricated herself from his hold and adjusted her dress. The crows settled back on the trees. The storks flew away across the river. Only the dogs barked.

"It sounded like a gunshot," she said nervously, trying to keep Juggut Singh from renewing his love-making. "Wasn't it from the village?"

"I don't know. Why are you trying to run away? It is all quiet now." Juggut Singh pulled her down beside him.

"This is no time for jesting. There is murder in the village. My father will get up and want to know where I have gone. I must get back at once."

"No, you will not. I won't let you. You can say you were with a girl friend."

"Don't talk like a stupid peasant. How . . . " Juggut Singh shut her mouth with his. He bore upon her with his enormous weight. Before she could free her arms he ripped open the cord of her trousers once again.

"Let me go. Let me . . . "

She could not struggle against Juggut Singh's brute force. She did not particularly want to. Her world was narrowed to the rhythmic sound of breathing and the warm smell of dusky skins raised to fever heat. His lips slubbered over her eyes and cheeks. His tongue sought the inside of her ears. In a state of frenzy she dug her nails into his thinly bearded cheeks and bit his nose. The stars above her went into a mad whirl and then came back to their places like a merry-go-round slowly coming to a stop. Life came back to its cooler, lower level. She felt the dead weight of the lifeless man; the sand gritting in her hair; the breeze trespassing on her naked limbs; the censorious stare of the myriads of stars. She pushed Juggut Singh away. He lay down beside her.

"That is all you want. And you get it. You are just a peasant. Always wanting to sow your seed. Even if the world were going to hell you would want to do that. Even when guns are being fired in the village. Wouldn't you?" she nagged.

"Nobody is firing any guns. Just your imagination," answered Juggut Singh wearily, without looking at her.

Faint cries of wailing wafted across to the riverside. The couple sat up to listen. Two shots rang out in quick succession. The crows flew out of the keekars, cawing furiously.

The girl began to cry.

"Something is happening in the village. My father will wake up and know I have gone out. He will kill me."

Juggut Singh was not listening to her. He did not know what to do. If his absence from the village was discovered, he would be in trouble with the police. That did not bother him as much as the trouble the girl would be in. She might not come again. She was saying so: "I will never come to see you again. If Allah forgives me this time, I will never do it again."

"Will you shut up or do I have to smack your face?"

The girl began to sob. She found it hard to believe this was the same man who had been making love to her a moment ago.

"Quiet! There is someone coming," whispered Juggut Singh, putting his heavy hand on her mouth.

The couple lay still, peering into the dark. The five men carrying guns and spears passed within a few yards of them. They had uncovered their faces and were talking.

"Dakoo! Do you know them?" the girl asked in a whisper.

"Yes," Juggut said, "The one with the torch is Malli." His face went tight. "That incestuous lover of his sister! I've told him a thousand times this was no time for dacoities. And now he has brought his gang to my village! I will settle this with him."

The dacoits went up to the river and then downstream toward the ford a couple of miles to the south. A pair of lapwings pierced the still night with startled cries: "Teet-tittee-tittee-whoot, tee-tee-whoot, tee-tee-whoot, tit-tit-tee-whoot."

"Will you report them to the police?"

Juggut Singh sniggered. "Let us get back before they miss me in the village."

The pair walked back toward Mano Majra, the man in front, the girl a few paces behind him. They could hear the sound of wailing and the barking of dogs. Women were shouting to each other across the roofs. The whole village seemed to be awake. Juggut Singh stopped near the pond and turned round to speak to the girl.

"Nooro, will you come tomorrow?" he asked, pleading.

"You think of tomorrow and I am bothered about my life. You have your good time even if I am murdered."

"No one can harm you while I live. No one in Mano Majra can raise his eyebrows at you and get away from Jugga. I am not a budmash for nothing," said he haughtily. "You tell me tomorrow what happens or the day after tomorrow when all this —whatever it is—is over. After the goods train?"

"No! No! No!" answered the girl. "What will I say to my father now? This noise is bound to have waked him."

"Just say you had gone out. Your stomach was upset or something like that. You heard the firing and were hiding till the dacoits had left. Will you come the day after tomorrow then?"

"No," she repeated, this time a little less emphatically. The excuse might work. Just as well her father was almost blind. He would not see her silk shirt, nor the antimony in her eyes. Nooran walked away into the darkness, swearing she would never come again.

Juggut Singh went up the lane to his house. The door was open. Several villagers were in the courtyard talking to his mother. He turned around quietly and made his way back to the river.

In bureaucratic circles Mano Majra has some importance because of an officers' rest house just north of the railway bridge. It is a flat-roofed bungalow made of khaki bricks with a verandah in front facing the river. It stands in the middle of a squarish plot enclosed by a low wall. From the gate to the verandah runs a road with a row of bricks to deckle-edge each side and mark it off from the garden. The garden is a pancake of plastered mud without a blade of grass to break its flat, even surface, but a few scraggy bushes of jasmine grow beside the columns of the verandah and near the row of servants' quarters at the rear of the house. The rest house was originally built for the engineer in charge of the construction of the bridge. After the completion of the bridge, it became the common property of all senior officers. Its popularity is due to its proximity to the river. All about it are wild wastes of pampas grass and dhak, or flame of the forest, and here partridges call to their mates from sunrise to sundown. When the river has receded to its winter channel, bulrushes grow in the marshes and ponds left behind. Geese, mallard, widgeon, teal, and many other kinds of waterfowl frequent these places, and the larger pools abound with rahu and malli and mahseer.

Throughout the winter months, officers arrange tours that involve a short halt at the Mano Majra rest house. They go for waterfowl at sunrise, for partridges during the day, fish in the afternoons, and once more for ducks when they come back in their evening flight. In spring the romantic come to ruminate—to sip their whisky and see the bright orange of the dhak shame the rich red hues of the sun setting over the river; to hear the soothing snore of frogs in the marshes and the rumble of trains that go by; to watch fireflies flitting among the reeds as the moon comes up from under the arches of the bridge. During the early months of summer, only those who are looking for solitude come to Mano Majra rest house. But once the monsoon breaks, the visitors multiply, for the swollen waters of the Sutlej are a grand and terrifying sight.

On the morning before the dacoity in Mano Majra, the rest house had been done up to receive an important guest. The sweeper had washed the bathrooms, swept the rooms, and sprinkled water on the road. The bearer and his wife had dusted and rearranged the furniture. The sweeper's boy had unwound the rope on the punkah which hung from the ceiling and put it through the hole in the wall so that he could pull it from the verandah. He had put on a new red loincloth and was sitting on the verandah tying and untying knots in the punkah rope. From the kitchen came the smell of currying chicken.

At eleven o'clock a subinspector of police and two constables turned up on bicycles to inspect the arrangements. Then two orderlies arrived. They wore white uniforms with red sashes round their waists and white turbans with broad bands in front. On the bands were pinned brass emblems of the government of the Punjab—the sun rising over five wavy lines representing the rivers of the province. With them were several villagers who carried the baggage and the glossy black official dispatch cases.

An hour later a large gray American car rolled in. An orderly stepped out of the front seat and opened the rear door for his master. The subinspector and the policemen came to attention and saluted. The villagers moved away to a respectful distance. The bearer opened the wire gauze door leading to the main bed- sitting room. Mr. Hukum Chand, magistrate and deputy commissioner of the district, heaved his corpulent frame out of the car. He had been traveling all morning and was somewhat tired and stiff. A cigarette perched on his lower lip sent a thin stream of smoke into his eyes. In his right hand he held a ciga-rette tin and a box of matches. He ambled up to the subinspector and gave him a friendly slap on the back while the other still stood at attention.

"Come along, Inspector Sahib, come in," said Hukum Chand. He took the inspector's right hand and led him into the room. The bearer and the deputy commissioner's personal servant fol-lowed. The constables helped the chauffeur to take the luggage out of the car.

Hukum Chand went straight into the bathroom and washed the dust off his face. He came back still wiping his face with a towel. The subinspector stood up again.

"Sit down, sit down," he commanded.

18

He flung the towel on his bed and sank into an armchair. The punkah began to flap forward and backward to the grating sound of the rope moving in the hole in the wall. One of the orderlies undid the magistrate's shoes and took off his socks and began to rub his feet. Hukum Chand opened the cigarette tin and held it out to the subinspector. The subinspector lit the magistrate's cigarette and then his own. Hukum Chand's style of smoking betrayed his lower-middle-class origin. He sucked noisily, his mouth glued to his clenched fist. He dropped cigarette ash by snapping his fingers with a flourish. The subinspector, who was a younger man, had a more sophisticated manner.

"Well, Inspector Sahib, how are things?"

The subinspector joined his hands. "God is merciful. We only pray for your kindness."

"No communal trouble in this area?"

"We have escaped it so far, sir. Convoys of Sikh and Hindu refugees from Pakistan have come through and some Muslims have gone out, but we have had no incidents."

"You haven't had convoys of dead Sikhs this side of the frontier. They have been coming through at Amritsar. Not one person living! There has been killing over there." Hukum Chand held up both his hands and let them drop heavily on his thighs in a gesture of resignation. Sparks flew off his cigarette and fell on his trousers. The subinspector slapped them to extinction with obsequious haste.

"Do you know," continued the magistrate, "the Sikhs retaliated by attacking a Muslim refugee train and sending it across the border with over a thousand corpses? They wrote on the engine 'Gift to Pakistan'!"

The subinspector looked down thoughtfully and answered: "They say that is the only way to stop killings on the other side. Man for man, woman for woman, child for child. But we Hindus are not like that. We cannot really play this stabbing game. When it comes to an open fight, we can be a match for any people. I believe our R.S.S. boys beat up Muslim gangs in all the cities. The Sikhs are not doing their share. They have lost their manliness. They just talk big. Here we are on the border with Muslims living in Sikh villages as if nothing had happened. Every morning and evening the muezzin calls for prayer in the heart of a village like Mano Majra. You ask the Sikhs why they allow it and they answer that the Muslims are their brothers. I am sure they are getting money from them."

Hukum Chand ran his fingers across his receding forehead into his hair.

"Any of the Muslims in this area well-to-do?"

"Not many, sir. Most of them are weavers or potters."

"But Chundunnugger is said to be a good police station. There are so many murders, so much illicit distilling, and the Sikh peasants are prosperous. Your predecessors have built themselves houses in the city."

"Your honor is making fun of me."

"I don't mind your taking whatever you do take, within reason of course—everyone does that—only be careful. This new government is talking very loudly of stamping out all this. After a few months in office their enthusiasm will cool and things will go on as before. It is no use trying to change things overnight."

"They are not the ones to talk. Ask anyone coming from Delhi and he will tell you that all these Gandhi disciples are minting money. They are as good saints as the crane. They shut their eyes piously and stand on one leg like a yogi doing penance; as soon as a fish comes near—hurrup."

Hukum Chand ordered the servant rubbing his feet to get some beer. As soon as they were alone, he put a friendly hand on the subinspector's knee.

"You talk rashly like a child. It will get you into trouble one day. Your principle should be to see everything and say nothing. The world changes so rapidly that if you want to get on you cannot afford to align yourself with any person or point of view. Even if you feel strongly about something, learn to keep silent."

The subinspector's heart warmed with gratitude. He wanted

to provoke more paternal advice by irresponsible criticism. He knew that Hukum Chand agreed with him.

"Sometimes, sir, one cannot restrain oneself. What do the Gandhi-caps in Delhi know about the Punjab? What is happening on the other side in Pakistan does not matter to them. They have not lost their homes and belongings; they haven't had their mothers, wives, sisters and daughters raped and murdered in the streets. Did your honor hear what the Muslim mobs did to Hindu and Sikh refugees in the market places at Sheikhupura and Gujranwala? Pakistan police and the army took part in the killings. Not a soul was left alive. Women killed their own children and jumped into wells that filled to the brim with corpses."

"Harey Ram, Harey Ram," rejoined Hukum Chand with a deep sigh. "I know it all. Our Hindu women are like that: so pure that they would rather commit suicide than let a stranger touch them. We Hindus never raise our hands to strike women, but these Muslims have no respect for the weaker sex. But what are we to do about it? How long will it be before it starts here?"

"I hope we do not get trains with corpses coming through Mano Majra. It will be impossible to prevent retaliation. We have hundreds of small Muslim villages all around, and there are some Muslim families in every Sikh village like Mano Majra," said the subinspector, throwing a feeler.

Hukum Chand sucked his cigarette noisily and snapped his fingers.

"We must maintain law and order," he answered after a pause. "If possible, get the Muslims to go out peacefully. Nobody really benefits by bloodshed. Bad characters will get all the loot and the government will blame us for the killing. No, Inspector Sahib, whatever our views—and God alone knows what I would have done to these Pakistanis if I were not a government servant—we must not let there be any killing or destruction of property. Let them get out, but be careful they do not take too much with them. Hindus from Pakistan were stripped of all their belongings before they were allowed to leave. Pakistani magistrates have become millionaires overnight. Some on our side have not done too badly either. Only where there was killing or burning the government suspended or transferred them. There must be no killing. Just peaceful evacuation."

The bearer brought a bottle of beer and put two glasses before Mr. Hukum Chand and the subinspector. The subinspector picked up his glass and put his hand over it, protesting, "No, sir, I could not be impertinent and drink in your presence."

The magistrate dismissed the protest peremptorily. "You will have to join me. It is an order. Bearer, fill the Inspector Sahib's glass and lay out lunch for him."

The subinspector held out his glass for the bearer to fill. "If you order me to, I cannot disobey." He began to relax. He took off his turban and put it on the table. It was not like a Sikh turban which needed re-tying each time it was taken off; it was just three yards of starched khaki muslin wrapped round a blue skullcap which could be put on and off like a hat.

"What is the situation in Mano Majra?"

"All is well so far. The Tambardar reports regularly. No refugees have come through the village yet. I am sure no one in Mano Majra even knows that the British have left and the country is divided into Pakistan and Hindustan. Some of them know about Gandhi but I doubt if anyone has ever heard of Jinnah."

"That is good. You must keep an eye on Mano Majra. It is the most important village on the border here. It is so close to the bridge. Are there any bad characters in the village?"

"Only one, sir. His name is Jugga. Your honor confined him to the village. He reports himself to the lambardar every day and comes to the police station once every week."

"Jugga? Which one is he?"

"You must remember Juggut Singh, son of the dacoit Alam Singh who was hanged two years ago. He is that very big fellow. He is the tallest man in this area. He must be six foot four —and broad. He is like a stud bull."

"Oh yes, I remember. What does he do to keep himself out of mischief? He used to come up before me in some case or other every month."

The subinspector smiled broadly. "Sir, what the police of the Punjab has failed to do, the magic of the eyes of a girl of sixteen has done."

Hukum Chand's interest was aroused.

"He has a liaison?" he asked.

"With a Muslim weaver's daughter. She is dark, but her eyes are darker. She certainly keeps Jugga in the village. And no one dares say a word against the Muslims. Her blind father is the mullah of the mosque."

The two drank their beer and smoked till the bearer brought in lunch. They continued drinking and eating and discussing the situation in the district till late in the afternoon. Beer and rich food made Hukum Chand heavy with sleep. Chicks on the verandah had been lowered to keep out the glare of the noonday sun. The punkah flapped gently to and fro with a weary plaintive creak. A feeling of numb drowsiness came over Hukum Chand. He got out his silver toothpick, picked his teeth and rubbed the toothpick on the tablecloth. Even that did not help him ward off sleep. The subinspector noticed the magistrate nodding and stood up to take leave.

"Have I your permission to leave, sir?"

"If you want to rest, you can find a bed here."

"You are very kind, sir, but I have a few things to attend to at the station. I will leave two constables here. If your honor desires my presence, they will inform me."

"Well," said the magistrate hesitantly, "have you made any arrangements for the evening?"

"Is it possible for me to have overlooked that? If she does not please you, you can have me dismissed from service. I will tell the driver where to go and collect the party."

The subinspector saluted and left. The magistrate stretched himself on the bed for a late afternoon siesta.

The sound of the car leaving the bungalow woke Hukum Chand from his sleep. Pampas-stalk chicks which hung on the verandah had been folded into large Swiss rolls and tied between the columns. The stark white of the verandah was mellowed in the soft amber of the setting sun. The sweeper boy lay curled on the brick floor clutching the punkah rope in his hand. His father was sprinkling water all around the rest house. The damp smell of earth mixed with the sweet odor of jasmines came through the wire gauze door. In front of the house, the servants had spread a large coir mat with a carpet on it. At one end of the carpet was a big cane chair, a table with a bottle of whisky, a couple of tumblers and plates of savories. Several bottles of soda water stood in a row beneath the table.

Hukum Chand shouted for his servant to get his bath ready and bring in hot water for shaving. He lit a cigarette and lay in bed staring at the ceiling. Just above his head two geckos were getting ready for a fight. They crawled toward each other emitting little rasping noises. They paused with half an inch between them and moved their tails with slow, menacing deliberation, then came to a head-on collision. Before Hukum Chand could move away they fell with a loud plop just beside his pillow. A cold clammy feeling came over him. He jumped out of bed and stared at the geckos. The geckos stared back at him, still holding onto each other by the teeth as if they were kissing. The bearer's footsteps broke the hypnotic stare with which the magistrate and the geckos had been regarding each other. The geckos ran down the bed and up the wall back to the ceiling. Hukum Chand felt as if he had touched the lizards and they had made his hands dirty. He rubbed his hands on the hem of his shirt. It was not the sort of dirt which could be wiped off or washed clean.

The bearer brought a mug of hot water and laid out the shaving gear on the dressing table. He put on a chair his master's clothes—a thin muslin shirt, a pair of baggy trousers strung with a peacock-blue silken cord interwoven with silver thread. He brushed the magistrate's black pumps till they shone and put them beside the chair.

Hukum Chand shaved and bathed with great care. After bathing he rubbed skin-lotion on his face and arms and dusted himself with perfumed talcum powder. He dabbed his fingers with eau de cologne. Brilliantine made his hair smooth and soggy and showed the white at the roots of it. He had not dyed it for a fortnight. He waxed his thick mustache and twirled it till the ends stifflly pointed to his eyes; the roots of his mustache also showed purple and white. He put on his thin muslin shirt through which his aertex vest showed clearly. The trousers fell in ordered starchy folds. He dabbed his clothes with a swab of cotton dipped in scent of musk rose. When he was ready he looked up at the ceiling. The geckos were there staring at him with their bright, black, pin-point eyes.

The American car drove back into the driveway. Hukum Chand went up to the wire gauze door still waxing his mustache. Two men and two women stepped out. One of the men carried a harmonium and the other a pair of drums. One of the women was old, with white hair dyed a rich henna-orange. The other was a young girl whose mouth was bloated with betel leaf and who wore a diamond glistening on one side of her flat nose. She carried a small bundle which jingled as she stepped out of the car. The party went and squatted on the carpet.

Hukum Chand carefully examined himself in the mirror. He noticed the white at the roots of his hair and smoothed it back again. He lit a cigarette and in his customary manner carried the tin of cigarettes with a matchbox on it. He half opened the wire gauze door and shouted for his bearer to bring the whisky, which he knew had already been put on the table. It was to warn the people outside of his coming. As he came out he let the door slam noisily. With slow deliberate steps punctuated by the creaking of his glossy pumps he walked up to the cane chair.

The party stood up to greet the magistrate. The two musicians salaamed, bowing their heads low. The old toothless woman broke into a sonorous singsong of praise: "May your fame and honor increase. May your pen write figures of thousands and hundreds of thousands." The young girl just stared at him with her large eyes lined with antimony and lampblack. The magistrate made a gesture with his hand ordering them to sit down. The old woman's voice came down to a whimper. All four sat down on the carpet.

The bearer poured out the whisky and soda for his master. Hukum Chand took a large gulp and wiped his mustache with the back of his hand. He twirled the pointed ends nervously. The girl opened her bundle and tied the ankle-bells round her ankles. The harmonium player played a single note. His companion beat the drums all round the edges with a tiny mallet and tightened and loosened the leather thongs by hammering the ring of wooden blocks wedged between them. He beat the taut white skin with his fingers till the drums were in key with the harmonium. The accompaniment was ready.

The young girl spat out the betel saliva and cleared her throat with a series of deep chesty coughs that brought up phlegm. The old woman spoke:

"Cherisher of the poor. What does your honor fancy? Something classical—pukka—or a love song?"

"No, nothing pukka. Something from the films. Some good film song—preferably Punjabi."

The young girl salaamed. "As you order."

The musicians put their heads together and after a brief consultation with the girl they began to play. The drums beat a preliminary tattoo and then softened down for the harmonium to join in. The two played for some time while the girl sat silently, looking bored and indifferent. When they finished the introductory piece, she blew her nose and cleared her throat again. She put her left hand on her ear and stretched the other toward the magistrate, addressing him in a shrill falsetto:

O lover mine, O lover that art gone,
I live but would rather die,
I see not for the tears that flow,
I breathe not, for I sigh.
As a moth that loves the flame,
By that flame is done to death,
Within myself have I lit a fire
That now robs me of my breath.
The nights I spend in counting stars,
The days in dreams of days to be
When homewards thou thy reins shall turn
Thy moon-fair face I again shall see.

The girl paused. The musicians started to play again for her to sing the refrain:

O letter, let my lover learn
How the fires of separation burn.

When the girl had finished her song, Hukum Chand flung a five-rupee note on the carpet. The girl and the musicians bowed their heads. The hag picked up the money and put it in her wallet, proclaiming: "May you ever rule. May your pen write hundreds of thousands. May . . ."

The singing began again. Hukum Chand poured himself a stiff whisky and drank it in one gulp. He wiped his mustache with his hand. He did not have the nerve to take a good look at the girl. She was singing a song he knew well; he had heard his daughter humming it:

In the breeze is flying
My veil of red muslin
Ho Sir, Ho Sir.

Hukum Chand felt uneasy. He took another whisky and dismissed his conscience. Life was too short for people to have consciences. He started to beat time to the song by snapping his fingers and slapping his thighs to each "Ho Sir. Ho Sir."

Twilight gave way to the dark of a moonless night. In the swamps by the river, frogs croaked. Cicadas chirped in the reeds. The bearer brought out a hissing paraffin lamp which cast a bright bluish light. The frame of the lamp threw a shadow over Hukum Chand. He stared at the girl who sat sheltered from the light. She was only a child and not very pretty, just young and unexploited. Her breasts barely filled her bodice. They could not have known the touch of a male hand. The thought that she was perhaps younger than his own daughter flashed across his mind. He drowned it quickly with another whisky. Life was like that. You took it as it came, shorn of silly conventions and values which deserved only lip worship. She wanted his money, and he . . . well. When all was said and done she was a prostitute and looked it. The silver sequins on her black sari sparkled. The diamond in her nose glittered like a star. Hukum Chand took another drink to dispel his remaining doubts. This time he wiped his mustache with his silk handkerchief. He began to hum louder and snapped his fingers with a flourish.

One film song followed another till all the Indian songs set to tunes of tangos and sambas that Hukum Chand knew were exhausted.

"Sing anything else you know," ordered the magistrate with lordly condescension. "Something new and gay."

The girl started to sing a song which had several English words in it:

Sunday after Sunday, O my life.

Hukum Chand exploded with an appreciative "wah, wah." When the girl finished her song, he did not throw the five-rupee note at her but asked her to come and take it from his hand. The old woman pushed the girl ahead.

"Go, the Government sends for you."

The girl got up and went to the table. She stretched out her hand to take the money; Hukum Chand withdrew his and put the note on his heart. He grinned lecherously. The girl looked at her companions for help. Hukum Chand put the note on the table. Before she could reach it he picked it up and again put it on his chest. The grin on his face became broader. The girl turned back to join the others. Hukum Chand held out the note for the third time.

"Go to the Government," pleaded the old woman. The girl turned round obediently and went to the magistrate. Hukum Chand put his arm round her waist.

"You sing well."

The girl gaped wide-eyed at her companions.

"The Government is talking to you. Why don't you answer him?" scolded the old woman. "Government, the girl is young and very shy. She will learn," she explained.

Hukum Chand put a glass of whisky to the girl's lips. "Drink a little. Just a sip for my sake," he pleaded.

The girl stood impassively without opening her mouth. The old woman spoke again.

"Government, she knows nothing about drink. She is hardly sixteen and completely innocent. She has never been near a man before. I have reared her for your honor's pleasure."

"Then she will eat something even if she does not drink," said Hukum Chand. He preferred to ignore the rest of the woman's speech. He picked up a meatball from a plate and tried to put it in the girl's mouth. She took it from him and ate it.

Hukum Chand pulled her onto his lap and began to play with her hair. It was heavily oiled and fixed in waves by gaudy celluloid hair-clips. He took out a couple of hairpins and loosened the bun at the back. The hair fell about her shoulders. The musicians and the old woman got up.

"Have we permission to leave?"

"Yes, go. The driver will take you home."

The old woman again set up a loud singsong: "May your fame and honor increase. May your pen write figures of thousands—nay, hundreds of thousands."

Hukum Chand produced a wad of notes and put it on the

table for her. Then the party went to the car, leaving the magistrate with the girl in his lap and the bearer waiting for orders.

"Shall I serve dinner, sir?"

"No, just leave the food on the table. We will serve ourselves. You can go." The bearer laid out the dinner and retired to his quarters.

Hukum Chand stretched out his hand and put out the paraffin lamp. It went out with a loud hiss, leaving the two in utter darkness save for a pale yellow light that flickered from the bedroom. Hukum Chand decided to stay out of doors.

The goods train had dropped the Mano Majra wagons and was leaving the station for the bridge. It came up noisily, its progress marked by the embers which flew out of the funnel of the engine. They were stoking coal in the firebox. A bright red-and-yellow light traveled through the spans of the bridge and was lost behind the jungle on the other side. The train's rumble got fainter and fainter. Its passing brought a feeling of privacy.

Hukum Chand helped himself to another whisky. The girl in his lap sat stiff and frigid.

"Are you angry with me? You don't want to talk to me?" asked Hukum Chand, pressing her closer to him. The girl did not answer nor look back at him.

The magistrate was not particularly concerned with her reactions. He had paid for all that. He brought the girl's face nearer his own and began kissing her on the back of her neck and on her ears. He could not hear the goods train any more. It had left the countryside in utter solitude. Hukum Chand could hear his breathing quicken. He undid the strap of the girl's bodice.

The sound of a shot shattered the stillness of the night The girl broke loose and stood up.

"Did you hear a shot?"

The girl nodded. "May be a shikari," she answered, speaking to him for the first time. She refastened her bodice.

"There can't be any shikar on a dark night."

The two stood in silence for some time—the man a little apprehensive; the girl relieved of the attentions of a lover whose breath smelled of whisky, tobacco and pyorrhea. But the silence told Hukum Chand that all was well. He took another whisky to make assurance doubly sure. The girl realized that there was no escape.

"Must be a cracker. Somebody getting married or something," said Hukum Chand, putting his arms round the girl. He kissed her on the nose. "Let us get married too," he added with a leer.

The girl did not answer. She allowed herself to be dragged onto the table amongst plates covered with stale meatballs and cigarette ash. Hukum Chand swept them off the table with his hand and went on with his love-making. The girl suffered his pawing without a protest. He picked her up from the table and laid her on the carpet amongst the litter of tumblers, plates and bottles. She covered her face with the loose end of her sari and turned it sideways to avoid his breath. Hukum Chand began fumbling with her dress.

From Mano Majra came sounds of people shouting and the agitated barking of dogs. Hukum Chand looked up. Two shots rang out and silenced the barking and shouting. With a loud oath Hukum Chand left the girl. She got up, brushing and adjusting her sari. From the servants' quarters the bearer and the sweeper came out carrying lanterns and talking excitedly. A little later the chauffeur drove the car into the driveway, its headlights lighting up the front of the bungalow.

The morning after the dacoity the railway station was more crowded than usual. Some Mano Majrans made a habit of being there to watch the 10:30 slow passenger train from Delhi to Lahore come in. They liked to see the few passengers who might get on or off at Mano Majra, and they also enjoyed endless arguments about how late the train was on a given day and when it had last been on time. Since partition of the country there had been an additional interest. Now the trains were often four or five hours late and sometimes as many as twenty. When they came, they were crowded with Sikh and Hindu refugees from Pakistan or with Muslims from India. People perched on the roofs with their legs dangling, or on bedsteads wedged in between the bogies. Some of them rode precariously on the buffers.

The train this morning was only an hour late—almost like prewar days. When it steamed in, the crying of hawkers on the platform and the passengers rushing about and shouting to each other gave the impression that many people would be getting off. But when the guard blew his whistle for departure, most of them were back on the train. Only a solitary Sikh peasant carrying an ironshod bamboo staff and followed by his wife with an infant resting on her hip remained with the hawkers on the platform. The man hoisted their rolled bedding onto his head and held it there with one hand. In the other he carried a large tin of clarified butter. The bamboo staff he held in his armpit, with one end trailing on the ground. Two green tickets stuck out beneath his mustache, which billowed from his upper lip onto his beard. The woman saw the line of faces peering through the iron railing of the station and drew her veil across her face. She followed her husband, her slippers sloshing on the gravel and her silver ornaments all ajingle. The stationmaster plucked the tickets from the peasant's mouth and let the couple out of the gate, where they were lost in a tumult of greetings and embraces.

The guard blew his whistle a second time and waved the green flag. Then, from the compartment just behind the engine, armed policemen emerged. There were twelve of them, and a subinspector. They carried rifles and their Sam Browne belts were charged with bullets. Two carried chains and handcuffs. From the other end of the train, near the guard's van, a young man stepped down. He wore a long white shirt, a brown waistcoat of coarse cotton, and loose pajamas, and he carried a holdall. He stepped gingerly off the train, pressing his tousled hair and looking all round. He was a small slight man, somewhat effeminate in appearance. The sight of the policemen emboldened him. He hoisted the holdall onto his left shoulder and moved jauntily toward the exit. The villagers watched the young man and the police party move from opposite directions toward the stationmaster who stood beside the gate. He had opened it wide for the police and was bowing obsequiously to the subinspector. The young man reached the gate first and stopped between the stationmaster and the police. The stationmaster quickly took the ticket from him, but the young man did not move on or make way for the subinspector.

"Can you tell me, Stationmaster Sahib, if there is a place I can stay in this village?"

The stationmaster was irritated. The visitor's urban accent, his appearance, dress and holdall had the stationmaster holding back his temper.

"There are no hotels or inns in Mano Majra," he answered with polite sarcasm. "There is only the Sikh temple. You will see the yellow flag-mast in the centre of the village."

"Thank you, sir."

The police party and the stationmaster scrutinized the youth with a little diffidence. Not many people said "thank you" in in these parts. Most of the "thank you" crowd were foreign-educated. They had heard of several well-to-do young men, educated in England, donning peasant garb to do rural uplift work. Some were known to be Communist agents. Some were sons of millionaires, some sons of high government officials. All were looking for trouble, and capable of making a lot of noise. One had to be careful.

The young man went out of the station toward the village. He walked with a consciously erect gait, a few yards in front of the policemen. He was uneasily aware of their attention. The itch on the back of his neck told him that they were looking at him and talking about him. He did not scratch or look back—he just walked on like a soldier. He saw the flag-mast draped in yellow cloth with a triangular flag above the conglomeration of mud huts. On the flag was the Sikh symbol in black, a quoit with a dagger running through and two swords crossed beneath. He went along the dusty path lined on either side by scraggy bushes of prickly pear which fenced it off from the fields. The path wound its narrow way past the mud huts to the opening in the center where the moneylender's house, the mosque and the temple faced each other. Underneath the peepul tree half a dozen villagers were sitting on a low wooden platform talking to each other. They got up as soon as they saw the policemen and followed them into Ram Lal's house. No one took any notice of the stranger.

He stepped into the open door of the temple courtyard. At the end opposite the entrance was a large hall in which the scripture, the Granth, lay wrapped in gaudy silks under a velvet awning. On one side were two rooms. A brick stairway ran along the wall to the roof of the rooms. Across the courtyard was a well with a high parapet. Beside the well stood a four-foot brick column supporting the long flag-mast with the yellow cloth covering it like a stocking.

The young man did not see anyone about. He could hear the sound of wet clothes being beaten on a slab of stone. He walked timidly to the other side of the well. An old Sikh got up with water dripping from his beard and white shorts.

"Sat Sri Akal."

"Sat Sri Akal."

"Can I stay for two or three days?"

"This is a gurdwara, the Guru's house—anyone may stay here. But you must have your head covered and you must not bring in any cigarettes or tobacco, nor smoke."

"I do not smoke," said the young man, putting the holdall on the ground and spreading his handkerchief on his head.

"No, Babu Sahib, only when you go in near the Book, the Granth Sahib, you take your shoes off and cover your head. Put your luggage in that room and make yourself comfortable. Will you have something to eat?"

"That is very kind of you. But I have brought my own food."

The old man showed the visitor to the spare room and then went back to the well. The young man went into the room. Its only furniture was a charpoy lying in the middle. There was a large colored calendar on one wall. It had a picture of the Guru on horseback with a hawk on one hand. Alongside the calendar were nails to hang clothes.

The visitor emptied his holdall. He took out his air mattress and blew it up on the charpoy. He laid out pajamas and a silk dressing gown on the mattress. He got out a tin of sardines, a tin of Australian butter and a packet of dry biscuits. He shook his water bottle. It was empty.

The old Sikh came to him, combing his long beard with his fingers.

"What is your name?" he asked, sitting down on the threshold.

"Iqbal. What is yours?"

"Iqbal Singh?" queried the old man. Without waiting for an answer, he continued. "I am the bhai of the temple. Bhai Meet Singh. What is your business in Mano Majra, Iqbal Singhji?"

The young man was relieved that the other had not gone on with his first question. He did not have to say what Iqbal he was. He could be a Muslim, Iqbal Mohammed. He could be a Hindu, Iqbal Chand, or a Sikh, Iqbal Singh. It was one of the few names common to the three communities. In a Sikh village, an Iqbal Singh would no doubt get a better deal, even if his hair was shorn and his beard shaved, than an Iqbal Mohammed or an Iqbal Chand. He himself had few religious feelings.

"I am a social worker, Bhaiji. There is much to be done in our villages. Now with this partition there is so much bloodshed going on someone must do something to stop it. My party has sent me here, since this place is a vital point for refugee movements. Trouble here would be disastrous."

The bhai did not seem interested in Iqbal's occupation.

"Where are you from, Iqbal Singhji?"

Iqbal knew that meant his ancestors and not himself.

35

"I belong to district Jhelum—now in Pakistan—but I have been in foreign countries a long time. It is after seeing the world that one feels how backward we are and one wants to do things about it. So I do social work."

"How much do they pay you?"

Iqbal had learned not to resent these questions.

"I don't get paid very much. Just my expenses."

"Do they pay the expenses of your wife and children also?"

"No, Bhaiji. I am not married. I really . . . "

"How old are you?"

"Twenty-seven. Tell me, do other social workers come to this village?" Iqbal decided to ask questions to stop Meet Singh's interrogation.

"Sometimes the American padres come."

"Do you like their preaching Christianity in your village?"

"Everyone is welcome to his religion. Here next door is a Muslim mosque. When I pray to my Guru, Uncle Imam Baksh calls to Allah. How many religions do they have in Europe?"

"They are all Christians of one kind or another. They do not quarrel about their religions as we do here. They do not really bother very much about religion."

"So I have heard," said Meet Singh ponderously. "That is why they have no morals. The sahibs and their wives go about with other sahibs and their wives. That is not good, is it?"

"But they do not tell lies like we do and they are not corrupt and dishonest as so many of us are," answered Iqbal.

He got out his tin opener and opened the tin of sardines. He spread the fish on a biscuit and continued to talk while he ate.

"Morality, Meet Singhji, is a matter of money. Poor people cannot afford to have morals. So they have religion. Our first problem is to get people more food, clothing, comfort. That can only be done by stopping exploitation by the rich, and abolishing landlords. And that can only be done by changing the government."

Meet Singh, with disgusted fascination, watched the young

man eating fish complete with head, eyes and tail. He did not pay much attention to the lecture on rural indebtedness, the average national income, and capitalist exploitation which the other poured forth with flakes of dry biscuits. When Iqbal had finished eating Meet Singh got up and brought him a tumbler of water from his pitcher. Iqbal did not stop talking. He only raised his voice when the bhai went out.

Iqbal produced a little packet of cellophane paper from his pocket, took a white pill from it and dropped it in the tumbler. He had seen Meet Singh's thumb, with its black crescent of dirt under the nail, dipping into the water. In any case it was out of a well which could never have been chlorinated.

"Are you ill?" asked the old man, seeing the other wait for the pill to dissolve.

"No, it helps me to digest my food. We city-dwellers need this sort of thing after meals."

Iqbal resumed his speech. "To add to it all," he continued, "there is the police system which, instead of safeguarding the citizen, maltreats him and lives on corruption and bribery. You know all about that, I am sure."

The old man nodded his head in agreement. Before he could comment, the young man spoke again. "A party of policemen with an inspector came over on the same train with me. They will no doubt eat up all the chickens, the inspector will make a little money in bribes, and they will move on to the next village. One would think they had nothing else to do but fleece people."

Reference to the police awaked the old man from his absent-minded listening. "So the police have come after all. I must go and see what they are doing. They must be at the moneylender's house. He was murdered last night, just across from the gurdwara. The dacoits took a lot of cash and they say over five thousand rupees in silver and gold ornaments from his women."

Meet Singh realized the interest he had created and slowly got up, repeating, "I should be going. All the village will be there. They will be taking the corpse for medical examination. If a man is killed he cannot be cremated till the doctor certifies him dead." The old man gave a wry smile.

"A murder! Why, why was he murdered?" stammered Iqbal, somewhat bewildered. He was surprised that Meet Singh had not mentioned the murder of a next-door neighbor all this time. "Was it communal? Is it all right for me to be here? I do not suppose I can do much if the village is all excited about a murder."

"Why, Babu Sahib, you have come to stop killing and you are upset by one murder?" asked Meet Singh, smiling. "I thought you had come to stop such things, Babu Sahib. But you are quite safe in Mano Majra," he added. "Dacoits do not come to the same village more than once a year. There will be another dacoity in another village in a few days and people will forget about this one. We can have a meeting here one night after the evening prayer and you can tell them all you want. You had better rest. I will come back and tell you what happens."

The old man hobbled out of the courtyard. Iqbal collected the empty tin, his knife and fork and tin plate, and took them to the well to wash.

In the afternoon, Iqbal stretched himself on the coarse string charpoy and tried to get some sleep. He had spent the night sitting on his bedroll in a crowded third-class compartment. Every time he had dozed off, the train had come to halt at some wayside station and the door was forced open and more peasants poured in with their wives, bedding and tin trunks. Some child sleeping in its mother's lap would start howling till its wails were smothered by a breast thrust into its mouth. The shouting and clamor would continue until long after the train had left the station. The same thing was repeated again and again, till the compartment meant for fifty had almost two hundred people in it, sitting on the floor, on seats, on luggage racks, on trunks, on bedrolls, and on each other, or standing in the corners. There were dozens outside perched precariously on footboards, holding onto the door handles. There were several people on the roof. The heat and smell were oppressive. Tempers were frayed and every few minutes an argument would start because someone had spread himself out too much or had trod on another's foot on his way to the lavatory. The argument would be joined on either side by friends or relatives and then by all the others trying to patch it up Iqbal had tried to read in the dim light speckled with shadows of moths that fluttered round the globe. He had hardly read a paragraph before his neighbor had observed:

"You are reading."

"Yes, I am reading."

"What are you reading?"

"A book."

It had not worked. The man had simply taken the book out of Iqbal's hand and turned over its pages.

"English?"

"Yes, English."

"You must be educated."

Iqbal did not comment.

The book had gone round the compartment for scrutiny. They had all looked at him. He was educated, therefore belonged to a different class. He was a babu.

"What honorable noun does your honor bear?"

"My name is Iqbal."

"May your Iqbal [fame] ever increase."

The man had obviously taken him to be a Muslim. Just as well. All the passengers appeared to be Muslims on their way to Pakistan.

"Where does your wealth reside, Babu Sahib?"

"My poor home is in Jhelum district," Iqbal had answered without irritation. The answer confirmed the likelihood of his being Muslim: Jhelum was in Pakistan.

Thereafter other passengers had joined in the cross-examination. Iqbal had to tell them what he did, what his source of income was, how much he was worth, where he had studied, why he had not married, all the illnesses he had ever suffered from. They had discussed their own domestic problems and diseases and had sought his advice. Did Iqbal know of any secret prescriptions or herbs that the English used when they were "rundown"? Iqbal had given up the attempt to sleep or read. They had kept up the conversation till the early hours of the morning. He would have described the journey as insufferable except that the limits to which human endurance could be stretched in India made the word meaningless. He had got off at Mano Majra with a sigh of relief. He could breathe the fresh air. He was looking forward to a long siesta.

But sleep would not come to Iqbal. There was no ventilation in the room. It had a musty earthy smell. A pile of clothes in the corner stank of stale clarified butter, and there were flies buzzing all round. Iqbal spread a handkerchief on his face. He could hardly breathe. With all that, just as he had managed to doze off, Meet Singh came in exclaiming philosophically:

"Robbing a fellow villager is like stealing from one's mother. Iqbal Singhji, this is Kalyug—the dark age. Have you ever heard of dacoits looting their neighbors' homes? Now all morality has left the world."

Iqbal removed the handkerchief from his face.

"What has happened?"

"What has happened?" repeated Meet Singh, feigning surprise. "Ask me what has not happened! The police sent for Jugga—Jugga is a budmash number ten [from the number of the police register in which names of bad characters are listed]. But Jugga had run away, absconded. Also, some of the loot—a bag of bangles—was found in his courtyard. So we know who did it. This is not the first murder he has committed—he has it in his blood. His father and grandfather were also dacoits and were hanged for murder. But they never robbed their own village folk. As a matter of fact, when they were at home, no dacoit dared come to Mano Majra. Juggut Singh has disgraced his family."

Iqbal sat up rubbing his forehead. His countrymen's code of morals had always puzzled him, with his anglicized way of looking at things. The Punjabi's code was even more baffling. For them truth, honor, financial integrity were "all right," but these were placed lower down the scale of values than being true to one's salt, to one's friends and fellow villagers. For friends, you could lie in court or cheat, and no one would blame you. On the contrary, you became a *nar admi*—a he-man who had defied authority (magistrates and police) and religion (oath on the scripture) but proved true to friendship. It was the projection of rural society where everyone in the village was a relation and loyalty to the village was the supreme test. What bothered Meet Singh, a priest, was not that Jugga had committed murder but that his hands were soiled with the blood of a fellow villager. If Jugga had done the same thing in the neighboring village, Meet Singh would gladly have appeared in his defense and sworn on the holy Granth that Jugga had been praying in the gurdwara at the time of the murder. Iqbal had wearied of talking to people like Meet Singh. They did not understand. He had come to the conclusion that he did not belong.

Meet Singh was disappointed that he had failed to arouse Iqbal's interest.

"You have seen the world and read many books, but take it from me that a snake can cast its slough but not its poison. This saying is worth a hundred thousand rupees."

Iqbal did not register appreciation of the valuable saying. Meet Singh explained: "Jugga had been going straight for some time. He plowed his land and looked after his cattle. He never left the village, and reported himself to the lambardar every day. But how long can a snake keep straight? There is crime in his blood."

"There is no crime in anyone's blood any more than there is goodness in the blood of others," answered Iqbal waking up.

41

This was one of his pet theories. "Does anyone ever bother to find out why people steal and rob and kill? No! They put them in jail or hang them. It is easier. If the fear of the gallows or the cell had stopped people from killing or stealing, there would be no murdering or stealing. It does not. They hang a man every day in this province. Yet ten get murdered every twenty-four hours. No, Bhaiji, criminals are not born. They are made by hunger, want and injustice."

Iqbal felt a little silly for coming out with these platitudes. He must check this habit of turning a conversation into a sermon. He returned to the subject.

"I suppose they will get Jugga easily if he is such a well-known character."

"Jugga cannot go very far. He can be recognized from a kos. He is an arm's length taller than anyone else. The Deputy Sahib has already sent orders to all police stations to keep a lookout for Jugga."

"Who is the Deputy Sahib?" asked Iqbal.

"You do not know the Deputy?" Meet Singh was surprised. "It's Hukum Chand. He is staying at the dak bungalow north of the bridge. Now Hukum Chand is a *nar admi*. He started as a foot-constable and see where he is now! He always kept the sahibs pleased and they gave him one promotion after another. The last one gave him his own place and made him Deputy. Yes, Iqbal Singhji, Hukum Chand is a *nar admi*—and clever. He is true to his friends and always gets things done for them. He has had dozens of relatives given good jobs. He is one of a hundred. Nothing counterfeit about Hukum Chand."

"Is he a friend of yours?"

"Friend? No, no," protested Meet Singh. "I am a humble bhai of the gurdwara and he is an emperor. He is the government and we are his subjects. If he comes to Mano Majra, you will see him."

There was a pause in the conversation. Iqbal slipped his feet into his sandals and stood up.

"I must take a walk. Which way do you suggest I should go?"

"Go in any direction you like. It is all the same open country. Go to the river. You will see the trains coming and going. If you cross the railroad track you will see the dak bungalow. Don't be too late. These are bad times and it is best to be indoors before dark. Besides, I have told the lambardar and Uncle Imam Baksh—he is mullah of the mosque—that you are here. They may be coming in to talk to you."

"No, I won't be late."

Iqbal stepped out of the gurdwara. There was no sign of activity now. The police had apparently finished investigating. Half a dozen constables lay sprawled on charpoys under the peepul tree. The door of Ram Lal's house was open. Some villagers sat on the floor in the courtyard. A woman wailed in a singsong which ended up in convulsions of crying in which other women joined. It was hot and still. The sun blazed on the mud walls.

Iqbal walked in the shade of the wall of the gurdwara. Children had relieved themselves all along it. Men had used it as a urinal. A mangy bitch lay on her side with a litter of eight skinny pups yapping and tugging at her sagging udders.

The lane ended abruptly at the village pond—a small patch of muddy water full of buffaloes with their heads sticking out.

A footpath skirted the pond and went along a dry watercourse through the wheat fields toward the river. Iqbal went along the watercourse watching his steps carefully. He reached the riverside just as the express from Lahore came up on the bridge. He watched its progress through the crisscross of steel. Like all the trains, it was full. From the roof, legs dangled down the sides onto the doors and windows. The doors and windows were jammed with heads and arms. There were people on buffers between the bogies. The two on the buffers on the tail end of the train were merrily kicking their legs and gesticulating. The train picked up speed after crossing the bridge. The engine driver started blowing the whistle and continued blowing till he had passed Mano Majra station. It was an expression of relief that they were out of Pakistan and into India.

Iqbal went up the riverbank toward the bridge. He was planning to go under it toward the dak bungalow when he noticed a Sikh soldier watching him from the sentry box at the end of the bridge. Iqbal changed his mind and walked boldly up to the rail embankment and turned toward Mano Majra station. The maneuver allayed the sentry's suspicion. Iqbal went a hundred yards up and then casually sat down on the railway line.

The passing express had waked Mano Majra from its late siesta. Boys threw stones at the buffaloes in the pond and drove them home. Groups of women went out in the fields and scattered themselves behind the bushes. A bullock cart carrying Ram Lal's corpse left the village and went toward the station. It was guarded by policemen. Several villagers went a little distance with it and then returned along with the relatives.

Iqbal stood up and looked all round. From the railway station to the roof of the rest house showing above the plumes of pampas, from the bridge to the village and back to the railway station, the whole place was littered with men, women, children, cattle, and dogs. There were kites wheeling high up in the sky, long lines of crows were flying from somewhere to somewhere, and millions of sparrows twittered about the trees. Where in India could one find a place which did not teem with life? Iqbal thought of his first reaction on reaching Bombay. Milling crowds —millions of them—on the quayside, in the streets, on railway platforms; even at night the pavements were full of people. The whole country was like an overcrowded room. What could you expect when the population went up by six every minute—five millions every year! It made all planning in industry or agriculture a mockery. Why not spend the same amount of effort in checking the increase in population? But how could you, in the land of the Kama sutra, the home of phallic worship and the son cult?

Iqbal was waked from his angry daydreaming by a shimmering sound along the steel wires which ran parallel to the railway lines. The signal above the sentry's box near the bridge came down. Iqbal stood up and brushed his clothes. The sun had gone down beyond the river. The russet sky turned gray as shades of twilight spread across the plain. A new moon looking like a finely pared finger nail appeared beside the evening star. The muezzin's call to prayer rose above the rumble of the approaching train.

Iqbal found his way back easily. All lanes met in the temple-mosque-moneylender's-house triangle with the peepul tree in the center. Sounds of wailing still came from Ram Lal's house. In the mosque, a dozen men stood in two rows silently going through their genuflections. In the gurdwara, Meet Singh, sitting beside the Book which was folded up in muslin on a cot, was reciting the evening prayer. Five or six men and women sat in a semicircle around a hurricane lantern and listened to him.

Iqbal went straight to his room and lay down on his charpoy in the dark. He had barely shut his eyes when the worshipers began to chant. The chanting stopped for a couple of minutes, only to start again. The ceremony ended with shouts of "Sat Sri Akal" and the beating of a drum. The men and women came out. Meet Singh held the lantern and helped them find their shoes. They started talking loudly. In the babel the only word Iqbal could make out was "babu." Somebody who had noticed Iqbal come in had told the others. There was some whispering and shuffling of feet and then silence.

Iqbal shut his eyes once more. A minute later Meet Singh stood on the threshold, holding the lantern.

"Iqbal Singhji, have you gone to bed without food? Would you like some spinach? I have also curd and buttermilk."

"No thank you, Bhaiji. I have the food I want."

"Our poor food . . . " started Meet Singh.

"No, no, it is not that," interrupted Iqbal sitting up, "it is just that I have it and it may be wasted if I don't eat it. I am a little tired and would like to sleep."

"Then you must have some milk. Banta Singh, the lambardar, is bringing you some. I will tell him to hurry up if you want to sleep early. I have another charpoy for you on the roof. It is too hot to sleep in here." Meet Singh left the hurricane lantern in the room and disappeared in the dark.

The prospect of having to talk to the lambardar was not very exciting. Iqbal fished out his silver hip flask from underneath the pillow and took a long swig of whisky. He ate a few dry biscuits that were in the paper packet. He took his mattress and pillow to the roof where a charpoy had been laid for him. Meet Singh apparently slept in the courtyard to guard the gurdwara.

Iqbal lay on his charpoy and watched the stars in the teeming sky until he heard several voices entering the gurdwara and coming up the stairs. Then he got up to greet the visitors.

"Sat Sri Akal, Babu Sahib."

"Salaam to you, Babu Sahib."

They shook hands. Meet Singh did not bother to introduce them. Iqbal pushed the air mattress aside to make room on the charpoy for the visitors. He sat down on the floor himself.

"I am ashamed for not having presented myself earlier," said the Sikh. "Please forgive me. I have brought some milk for you."

"Yes, Sahib, we are ashamed of ourselves. You are our guest and we have not rendered you any service. Drink the milk before it gets cold," added the other visitor. He was a tall lean man with a clipped beard.

"It is very kind of you . . . I know you have been busy with the police . . . I don't drink milk. Really I do not. We city-dwellers . . . "

The lambardar ignored Iqbal's well-mannered protests. He removed his dirty handkerchief from a large brass tumbler and began to stir the milk with his forefinger. "It is fresh. I milked the buffalo only an hour back and got the wife to boil it. I know

46

you educated people only drink boiled milk. There is quite a lot of sugar in it; it has settled at the bottom," he added with a final stir. To emphasize the quality of the milk, he picked up a slab of clotted cream on his forefinger and slapped it back in the milk.

"Here, Babuji, drink it before it gets cold."

"No! No! No, thank you, no!" protested Iqbal. He did not know how to get out of his predicament without offending the visitors. "I don't ever drink milk. But if you insist, I will drink it later. I like. it cold."

"Yes, you drink it as you like, Babuji," said the Muslim, coming to his rescue. "Banta Singh, leave the tumbler here. Bhai will bring it back in the morning."

The lambardar covered the tumbler with his handkerchief and put it under Iqbal's charpoy. There was a long pause. Iqbal had pleasant visions of pouring the milk with all its clotted cream down the drain.

"Well, Babuji," began the Muslim. "Tell us something. What is happening in the world? What is all this about Pakistan and Hindustan?"

"We live in this little village and know nothing," the lambardar put in. "Babuji, tell us, why did the English leave?"

Iqbal did not know how to answer simple questions like these. Independence meant little or nothing to these people. They did not even realize that it was a step forward and that all they needed to do was to take the next step and turn the make-believe political freedom into a real economic one.

"They left because they had to. We had hundreds of thousands of young men trained to fight in the war. This time they had the arms too. Haven't you heard of the mutiny of the Indian sailors? The soldiers would have done the same thing. The English were frightened. They did not shoot any of the Indians who joined the Indian National Army set up by the Japanese, because they thought the whole country would turn against them."

Iqbal's thesis did not cut much ice.

"Babuji, what you say may be right," said the lambardar hesitantly. "But I was in the last war and fought in Mesopotamia and Gallipoli. We liked English officers. They were better than the Indian."

"Yes," added Meet Singh, "my brother who is a havildar says all sepoys are happier with English officers than with Indian. My brother's colonel's mem-sahib still sends my niece things from London. You know, Lambardar Sahib, she even sent money at her wedding. What Indian officers' wives will do that?"

Iqbal tried to take the offensive. "Why, don't you people want to be free? Do you want to remain slaves all your lives?"

After a long silence the lambardar answered: "Freedom must be a good thing. But what will we get out of it? Educated people like you, Babu Sahib, will get the jobs the English had. Will we get more lands or more buffaloes?"

"No," the Muslim said. "Freedom is for the educated people who fought for it. We were slaves of the English, now we will be slaves of the educated Indians—or the Pakistanis."

Iqbal was startled at the analysis.

"What you say is absolutely right," he agreed warmly. "If you want freedom to mean something for you—the peasants and workers—you have to get together and fight. Get the banian Congress government out. Get rid of the princes and the land-lords and freedom will mean for you just what you think it should. More land, more buffaloes, no debts."

"That is what that fellow told us," interrupted Meet Singh, "that fellow . . . Lambardara, what was his name? Comrade Something-or-other. Are you a comrade, Babu Sahib?"

"No."

"I am glad. That comrade did not believe in God. He said when his party came into power they would drain the sacred pool round the temple at Turun Tarun and plant rice in it. He said it would be more useful."

"That is foolish talk," protested Iqbal. He wished Meet Singh had remembered the comrade's name. The man should be reported to headquarters and taken to task.

"If we have no faith in God then we are like animals," said the Muslim gravely. "All the world respects a religious man. Look at Gandhi! I hear he reads the Koran Sharif and the Unjeel along with his Vedas and Shastras. People sing his praise in the four corners of the earth. I have seen a picture in a newspaper of Gandhi's prayer meeting. It showed a lot of white men and women sitting cross-legged. One white girl had her eyes shut. They said she was the Big Lord's daughter. You see, Meet Singha, even the English respect a man of religion."

"Of course, Chacha. Whatever you say is right to the sixteenth anna of the rupee," agreed Meet Singh, rubbing his belly.

Iqbal felt his temper rise. "They are a race of four-twenties," he said vehemently. [Section 420 of the Indian Penal Code defines the offense of cheating.] "Do not believe what they say."

Once again he felt his venom had missed its mark. But the Big Lord's daughter sitting cross-legged with her eyes shut for the benefit of press photographers, and the Big Lord himself— the handsome, Hindustani-speaking cousin of the King, who loved India like the missionaries—was always too much for Iqbal.

"I have lived in their country many years. They are nice as human beings. Politically they are the world's biggest four-twenties. They would not have spread their domain all over the world if they had been honest. That, however, is irrelevant," added Iqbal. It was time to change the subject. "What is important is: what is going to happen now?"

"We know what is happening," the lambardar answered with some heat. "The winds of destruction are blowing across the land. All we hear is kill, kill. The only ones who enjoy freedom are thieves, robbers and cutthroats." Then he added calmly: "We were better off under the British. At least there was security."

There was an uneasy silence. An engine was shunting up and down the railway line rearranging its load of goods wagons. The Muslim changed the subject.

"That is the goods train. It must be late. Babu Sahib, you are tired; we must let you rest. If you need us, we will be always at your service."

They all got up. Iqbal shook hands with his visitors without showing any trace of anger. Meet Singh conducted the lambardar and the Muslim down to the courtyard. He then retired to his charpoy there.

Iqbal lay down once more and gazed at the stars. The wail of the engine in the still vast plain made him feel lonely and depressed. What could he—one little man—do in this enormous impersonal land of four hundred million? Could he stop the killing? Obviously not. Everyone—Hindu, Muslim, Sikh, Congressite, Leaguer, Akali, or Communist—was deep in it. It was fatuous to suggest that the bourgeois revolution could be turned into a proletarian one. The stage had not arrived. The proletariat was indifferent to political freedom for Hindustan or Pakistan, except when it could be given an economic significance like grabbing land by killing an owner who was of a different religious denomination. All that could be done was to divert the kill-and-grab instinct from communal channels and turn it against the propertied class. That was the proletarian revolution the easy way. His party bosses would not see it.

Iqbal wished they had sent someone else to Mano Majra. He would be so much more useful directing policy and clearing the cobwebs from their minds. But he was not a leader. He lacked the qualifications. He had not fasted. He had never been in jail. He had made none of the necessary "sacrifices." So, naturally, nobody would listen to him. He should have started his political career by finding an excuse to court imprisonment. But there was still time. He would do that as soon as he got back to Delhi. By then, the massacres would be over. It would be quite safe.

The goods train had left the station and was rumbling over the bridge. Iqbal fell asleep dreaming of a peaceful life in jail.

Early next morning, Iqbal was arrested.

Meet Singh had gone out to the fields carrying his brass mug of water and chewing a keekar twig he used as a toothbrush. Iqbal had slept through the rumble of passing trains, the muezzin's call, and the other village noises. Two constables came into the gurdwara, looked in his room, examined his celluloid cups and saucers, shining aluminum spoons, forks and knives, his thermos, and then came up onto the roof. They shook Iqbal rudely. He sat up rubbing his eyes, somewhat bewildered. Before he could size up the situation and formulate the curt replies he would like to have given, he had told the policemen his name and occupation. One of them filled in the blank spaces on a yellow piece of printed paper and held it in front of Iqbal's blinking eyes.

"Here is a warrant for your arrest. Get up."

The other slipped the ring at one end of a pair of handcuffs in his belt and unlocked the links to put round Iqbal's wrists. The sight of the handcuffs brought Iqbal wide awake. He jumped out of bed and faced the policemen.

"You have no right to arrest me like this," he shouted. "You made up the warrant in front of me. This is not going to end here. The days of police rule are over. If you dare put your hands on me, the world will hear about it. I will see that the papers tell the people how you chaps do your duty."

The policemen were taken aback. The young man's accent, the rubber pillows and mattress and all the other things they had seen in the room, and above all, his aggressive attitude, made them uneasy. They felt that perhaps they had made a mistake.

"Babu Sahib, we are only doing our duty. You settle this with the magistrate," one of them answered politely. The other fumbled uneasily with the handcuffs.

"I will settle it with the whole lot of you—police and magistrates! Come and disturb people in sleep! You will regret this mistake." Iqbal waited for the policemen to say something so that he could go on with his tirade against law and order. But they had been subdued.

"You will have to wait. I have to wash and change and leave my things in somebody's care," said Iqbal aggressively, giving them another chance to say something.

"All right, Babu Sahib. Take as long as you like."

The policemen's civil attitude deflated Iqbal's anger. He collected his things and went down the stairs to his room. He went to the well, pulled up a bucket of water and began to wash. He was in no hurry.

Bhai Meet Singh çame back vigorously brushing his teeth with the end of the keekar twig which he had chewed into a fibrous brush. The presence of policemen in the gurdwara did not surprise him. Whenever they came to the village and could not find accommodation at the lambardar's house they came to the temple. He had been expecting them after the money-lender's murder.

"Sat Sri Akal," said Meet Singh, throwing away his keekar toothbrush.

"Sat Sri Akal," replied the policemen.

"Would you like some tea or something? Some buttermilk?"

"We are waiting for the Babu Sahib," the policemen said. If you can give us something while he is getting ready, it will be very kind."

Meet Singh maintained a casual indifference. It was not up to him to argue with the police or be nosy about their business. Iqbal Singh was probably a "comrade." He certainly talked like one.

"I will make some tea for him, too," replied Meet Singh. He

looked at Iqbal. "Or will you have your own out of the big bottle?"

"Thank you very much," answered Iqbal through the tooth paste froth in his mouth. He spat it out. "The tea in the bottle must be cold by now. I would be grateful for a hot cup. And would you mind looking after my things while I am away? They are arresting me for something. They do not know themselves for what."

Meet Singh pretended he had not heard. The policemen looked a little sheepish.

"It is not our fault, Babu Sahib," one of them said. "Why are you getting angry with us? Get angry with the magistrate."

Iqbal ignored their protest by more brushing of his teeth. He washed his face and came back to the room rubbing himself with a towel. He let the air out of the mattress and the pillow and rolled them up. He emptied the holdall of its contents: books, clothes, torch, a large silver hip flask. He made a list of his things and put them back. When Meet Singh brought tea Iqbal handed him the holdall.

"Bhaiji, I have put all my things in the holdall. I hope it will not be too much trouble looking after them. I would rather trust you than the police in this free country of ours."

The policemen looked away. Meet Singh was embarrassed.

"Certainly, Babu Sahib," he said meekly. "I am your servant as well as that of the police. Here everyone is welcome. You like tea in your own cup?"

Iqbal got out his celluloid teacup and spoon. The constables took brass tumblers from Meet Singh. They wrapped the loose ends of their turbans round the tumblers to protect their hands from the hot brass. To reassure themselves they sipped noisily. But Iqbal was in complete possession of the situation. He sat on the string cot while they sat on the threshold and Meet Singh on the floor outside. They did not dare to speak to him for fear of rudeness. The constable with the handcuffs had quietly taken them off his belt and thrust them in his pocket. They finished their tea and looked up uneasily. Iqbal sat sullenly staring over their heads with an intensity charged with importance. He glared vacantly into space, occasionally taking a spinsterish sip of his tea. When he had finished, he stood up abruptly.

"I am ready," he announced, dramatically holding out his hands. "Put on the handcuffs."

"There is no need for handcuffs, Babuji," answered one of the constables. "You had better cover your face or you will be recognized at the identification parade."

Iqbal pounced on the opportunity. "Is this how you do your duty? If the rule is that I have to be handcuffed, then handcuffed I shall be. I am not afraid of being recognized. I am not a thief or a dacoit. I am a political worker. I will go through the village as I am so that people can see what the police do to people they do not like."

This outburst was too much for one of the constables. He spoke sharply:

"Babuji, we are being polite to you. We keep saying 'ji,' 'ji' to you all the time, but you want to sit on our heads. We have told you a hundred times we are doing our duty, but you insist on believing that we have a personal grudge." He turned to his colleague. "Put the handcuffs on the fellow. He can do what he likes with his face. If I had a face like his, I would want to hide it. We will report that he refused to cover it."

Iqbal did not have a ready answer to the sarcasm. He had a Semitic consciousness of his hooked nose. Quite involuntarily he brushed it with the back of his hand. Reference to his physical appearance always put him off. The handcuffs were fastened round his wrists and chained onto the policeman's belt.

"Sat Sri Akal, Bhaiji. I will be back soon."

"Sat Sri Akal, Iqbal Singhji, and may the Guru protect you. Sat Sri Akal, Sentryji."

"Sat Sri Akal."

The party marched out of the temple courtyard, leaving Meet Singh standing with the kettle of tea in his hand.

At the time the two constables were sent to arrest Iqbal, a posse of ten men was sent to arrest Juggut Singh. Policemen surrounded his house at all points. Constables armed with rifles were posted on neighboring roofs and in the front and rear of the house. Then six others armed with revolvers rushed into the courtyard. Juggut Singh lay on his charpoy, wrapped from head to foot in a dirty white sheet and snoring lustily. He had spent two nights and a day in the jungle without food or shelter. He had come home in the early hours of the morning when he believed everyone in the village would be asleep. The neighbors had been vigilant and the police were informed immediately. They waited till he had filled himself with food and was sound asleep. His mother had gone out, bolting the door from the outside.

Juggut Singh's feet were put in fetters and handcuffs were fastened on his right wrist while he slept. Policemen put their revolvers in their holsters. Men with rifles joined them in the courtyard. They prodded Juggut Singh with the butt ends of their guns.

"O Jugga, get up, it is almost afternoon."

"See how he sleeps like a pig without a care in the world."

Jugga sat up wearily, blinking his eyes. He gazed at the handcuffs and the fetters with philosophic detachment, then stretched his arms wide and yawned loudly. Sleep came on him again and he began to nod.

Juggut Singh's mother came in and saw her courtyard full of armed policemen. Her son sat on the charpoy with his head resting on his manacled hands. His eyes were shut. She ran up to him and clasped him by the knees. She put her head in his lap and started to cry.

Juggut Singh woke up from his reverie. He pushed his mother back rudely.

"Why are you crying?" he said. You know I had nothing to do with the dacoity."

She began to wail. "He did not do it. He did nothing. In the name of God, I swear he did nothing."

"Then where was he on the night of the murder?" the head constable said.

"He was out in his fields. He was not with the dacoits. I swear he was not."

"He is a budmash under orders not to go out of the village after sunset. We have to arrest him for that in any case." He motioned to his men. "Search the rooms and the barn." The head constable had his doubts about Juggut Singh partaking in a dacoity in his own village. It was most unusual.

Four constables busied themselves looking around the house, emptying steel trunks and tin cans. The haystack was pulled down and the hay scattered in the yard. The spear was found without difficulty.

"I suppose this has been put here by your uncle?" said the head constable addressing the mother sourly. "Wrap the blade in a piece of cloth, it may have blood stains on it."

"There is nothing on it," cried the mother, "nothing. He keeps it to kill wild pigs that come to destroy the crops. I swear he is innocent."

"We will see. We will see," the head constable dismissed her. "You better get proof of his innocence ready for the magistrate."

The old woman stopped moaning. She did have proof—the packet of broken bangles. She had not told Jugga about it. If she had, he would certainly have gone mad at the insult and been violent to someone. Now he was in fetters and handcuffs, he could only lose his temper.

"Wait, brother policeman. I have the evidence."

The policemen watched the woman go in and bring out a packet from the bottom of her steel trunk. She unwrapped the brown paper. There were broken pieces of blue and red glass bangles with tiny gold spots. Two of them were intact. The head constable took them.

"What sort of proofs are these?"

"The dacoits threw them in the courtyard after the murder. They wanted to insult Jugga for not coming with them. Look!" She held out her hands. "I am too old to wear glass bangles and they are too small for my wrists."

"Then Jugga must know who the dacoits were. What did they say when they threw them?" asked the head constable.

"Nothing, they said nothing. They abused Jugga . . . "

"Can't you keep your mouth shut?" interrupted Jugga angrily. "I do not know who the dacoits were. All I know is that I was not with them."

"Who leaves you bangles?" asked the head constable. He smiled and held up the bits of glass in his hands.

Jugga lost his temper. He raised his manacled fists and brought them heavily down on the head constable's palms. "What seducer of his mother can throw bangles at me? What . . . "

The constables closed round Juggut Singh and started slapping him and kicking him with their thick boots. Jugga sat down on his haunches, covering his head with his arms. His mother began to beat her forehead and started crying again. She broke into the cordon of policemen and threw herself on her son.

"Don't hit him. The Guru's curse be on you. He is innocent. It is all my fault. You can beat me."

The beating stopped. The head constable picked pieces of glass out of his palm, pressed out blood, and wiped it with his handkerchief.

"You keep the evidence of your son's innocence," he said bitterly. "We will get the story out of this son of a bitch of yours in our own way. When he gets a few lashes on his buttocks, he will talk. Take him out."

Juggut Singh was led out of the house in handcuffs and fetters.

He left without showing a trace of emotion for his mother, who continued to wail and beat her forehead and breasts. His parting words were:

"I will be back soon. They cannot give me more than a few months for having a spear and going out of the village. Sat Sri Akal."

Jugga recovered his temper as quickly as he had lost it. He forgot the incident of the bangles and the beating as soon as he stepped across his threshold. He had no malice or ill will toward the policemen: they were not human like other human beings. They had no affections, no loyalties or enmities. They were just men in uniforms you tried to avoid.

There was not much point in Juggut Singh covering his face. The whole village knew him. He went past the villagers, smiling and raising his manacled hands in a greeting to everyone. The fetters round his feet forced him to walk slowly with his legs apart. He had a devil-may-care jauntiness in his step. He showed his unconcern by twirling his thin brown mustache and cracking obscene jokes with the policemen.

Iqbal and the two constables joined Juggut Singh's party by the river. They all proceeded upstream toward the bridge. The head constable walked in front. Armed policemen marched on the sides and at the rear of the prisoners. Iqbal was lost in the khaki and red of their uniforms. Juggut Singh's head and shoulders showed above the turbans of the policemen. It was like a procession of horses with an elephant in their midst— taller, broader, slower, with his chains clanking like ceremonial trappings.

No one seemed to be in the mood to talk. The policemen were uneasy. They knew that they had made a mistake, or rather, two mistakes. Arresting the social worker was a blunder and a likely source of trouble. His belligerent attitude confirmed his innocence. Some sort of case would have to be made up against him. That was always a tricky thing to do to educated people. Juggut Singh was too obvious a victim to be the correct one. He had undoubtedly broken the law in leaving the village at night, but he was not likely to have joined in a dacoity in his own village. He would be too easily recognized by his enormous size. Also, it was quite clear that these two had met for the first time.

Iqbal's pride had been injured. Up to the time he met Juggut Singh, he was under the impression that he had been arrested for his politics. He had insisted on being handcuffed so that the villagers could see with what dignity he bore himself. They would be angered at such an outrage to civil liberties. But the men had gaped stupidly and the women peered through their veils and asked each other in whispers, "Who is this?" When he joined the group that escorted Juggut Singh, the point of the policeman's advice "Cover your face, otherwise you may be recognized at the identification parade," came home to him. He was under arrest in connection with the murder of Ram Lal. It was so stupid he could hardly believe it. Everyone knew that he had come to Mano Majra after the murder. On the same train as the policemen, in fact. They could be witness of his alibi. The situation was too ludicrous for words. But Punjabi policemen were not the sort who admitted making mistakes. They would trump up some sort of charge: vagrancy, obstructing officers in doing their duty, or some such thing. He would fight them tooth and nail.

The only one in the party who did not seem to mind was Juggut Singh. He had been arrested before. He had spent quite as much time in jail as at home. His association with the police was an inheritance. Register number ten at the police station, which gave the record of the activities of the bad characters of the locality, had carried his father Alam Singh's name while he lived. Alam Singh had been convicted of dacoity with murder, and hanged. Juggut Singh's mother had to mortgage all their land to pay lawyers. Juggut Singh had to find money to redeem the land, and he had done that within the year. No one could prove how he had raised the money, but at the end of the year the police had taken him. His name was entered in register number ten and he was officially declared a man of bad character. Behind his back everyone referred to him as a "number ten."

Juggut Singh looked at the prisoner beside him several times. He wanted to start a conversation. Iqbal had his eyes fixed in front of him and walked with the camera-consciousness of an actor facing the lens. Juggut Singh lost patience.

"Listen. What village are you from?" he asked and grinned, baring a set of even teeth studded with gold points in the centers.

Iqbal looked up, but did not return the smile.

"I am not a villager. I come from Delhi. I was sent to organize peasants, but the government does not like the people to be organized."

Juggut Singh became polite. He gave up the tone of familiarity. "I hear we have our own rule now," he said. "It is Mahatma Gandhi's government in Delhi, isn't it? They say so in our village."

"Yes, the Englishmen have gone but the rich Indians have taken their place. What have you or your fellow villagers got out of independence? More bread or more clothes? You are in the same handcuffs and fetters which the English put on you. We have to get together and rise. We have nothing to lose but these chains." Iqbal emphasized the last sentence by raising his hands up to his face and jerking them as if the movement would break the handcuffs.

The policemen looked at each other.

Juggut Singh looked down at the fetters round his ankles and the iron bars which linked them to the handcuffs.

"I am a budmash. All governments put me in jail."

"But," interrupted Iqbal angrily, "what makes you budmash? The government! It makes regulations and keeps registers, policemen and jailers to enforce them. For anyone they do not like, they have a rule which makes him a bad character and a criminal. What have I . . . "

"No, Babu Sahib," broke in Juggut Singh good-humoredly,

"it is our fate. It is written on our foreheads and on the lines of our hands. I am always wanting to do something. When there is plowing to be done or the harvest to be gathered, then I am busy. When there is no work, my hands still itch to do something. So I do something, and it is always wrong."

The party passed under the bridge and approached the rest house. Juggut Singh's complacency had put Iqbal off. He did not want to waste his breath arguing with a village bad character. He wanted to save his words for the magistrate. He would let him have it in English—the accent would make him squirm.

When the police brought in the prisoners, the subinspector ordered them to be taken to the servants' quarters. The magistrate was in his room dressing. The head constable left the prisoners with his men and came back to the bungalow.

"Who is this small chap you have brought?" asked the subinspector, looking a little worried.

"I arrested him on your orders. He was the stranger staying at the Sikh temple."

The answer irritated the subinspector. "I do not suppose you have any brains of your own! I leave a little job to you and you go and make a fool of yourself. You should have seen him before arresting him. Isn't he the same man who got off the train with us yesterday?"

"The train?" queried the head constable, feigning ignorance. "I did not see him on the train, cherisher of the poor. I only carried out your orders and arrested the stranger loitering about the village under suspicious circumstances."

The subinspector's temper shot up.

"Ass!"

The head constable avoided his officer's gaze.

"You are an ass of some place," he repeated with greater vehemence. Have you no brains at all?"

"Cherisher of the poor, what fault have I . . . "

"Shut up!"

The head constable started looking at his feet. The subinspector let his temper cool. He had to face Hukum Chand, who relied on him and did not expect to be let down. After some thought, the subinspector peered through the wire gauze door.

"Have I permission to enter?"

"Come in. Come in, Inspector Sahib," Hukum Chand replied. "Do not wait on formalities."

The subinspector went in, and saluted.

"Well, what have you been doing?" asked the magistrate. He was rubbing cream on his freshly shaven chin. In a tumbler on the dressing table a flat white tablet danced about the bottom, sending up a stream of bubbles.

"Sir, we have made two arrests this morning. One is Jugga budmash. He was out of his house on the night of the dacoity. We are bound to get some information out of him. The other is the stranger whose presence had been reported by the headman and you ordered him to be arrested."

Hukum Chand stopped rubbing his chin. He detected the attempt to pass off the second arrest onto him.

"Who is he?"

The subinspector shouted to the head constable outside.

"What is the name of the fellow you arrested at the Sikh temple?"

"Iqbal."

"Iqbal what?" questioned the magistrate loudly.

"I will just find out, sir." The head constable ran across to the servants' quarters before the magistrate could let fly at him. Hukum Chand felt his temper rising. He took a sip out of his glass. The subinspector shuffled uneasily. The head constable came back a few minutes later and coughed to announce his return.

"Sir." He coughed again. "Sir, he can read and write. He is educated."

The magistrate turned to the door angrily.

"Has he a father and mother, a faith, or not? Educated!"

"Sir," faltered the head constable, "he refuses to tell us his father's name and says he has no religion. He says he will speak to you himself."

"Go and find out," roared the magistrate. "Whip him on his buttocks till he talks. Go . . . no, wait, the Subinspector Sahib will handle this."

Hukum Chand was in a rage. He gulped down the fizzing water in the tumbler and mopped his head with the shaving towel. A belch relieved him of his mounting wrath.

"Nice fellows you and your policemen! You go and arrest people without finding out their names, parentage or caste. You make me sign blank warrants of arrest. Some day you will arrest the Governor and say Hukum Chand ordered you to do so. You will have me dismissed."

"Cherisher of the poor, I will go and look into this. This man came to Mano Majra yesterday. I will find out his antecedents and business."

"Well, then, go and find out, and do not just stand and stare," barked Hukum Chand. He was not in the habit of losing his temper or of being rude. After the subinspector had left, he examined his tongue in the mirror and put another tablet of seltzer in the tumbler.

The subinspector went out and stopped on the verandah to take a few deep breaths. The magistrate's wrath decided his attitude. He would have to take a strong line and finish the shilly-shallying. He went to the servants' quarters. Iqbal and his escort stood apart from Juggut Singh's crowd. The young man had a look of injured dignity. The subinspector thought it best not to speak to him.

"Search this man's clothes. Take him inside one of the quarters and strip him. I will examine them myself."

Iqbal's planned speech remained undelivered. The constable almost dragged him by the handcuffs into a room. His resistance had gone. He took off his shirt and handed it to the policeman. The subinspector came in and without bothering to examine the shirt ordered:

"Take off your pajamas!"

Iqbal felt humiliated. There was no fight left in him. "There are no pockets to the pajamas. I cannot hide anything in them."

"Take them off and do not argue." The subinspector slapped his khaki trousers with his swagger stick to emphasize the order.

Iqbal loosened the knot in the cord. The pajamas fell in a heap around his ankles. He was naked save for the handcuffs on his wrists. He stepped out of the pajamas to let the policemen examine them.

"No, that is not necessary," broke in the subinspector. "I have seen all I wanted to see. You can put on your clothes. You say you are a social worker. What was your business in Mano Majra?"

"I was sent by my party," answered Iqbal, re-tying the knot in the cord of his pajamas.

"What party?"

"People's Party of India."

The subinspector looked at Iqbal with a sinister smile. "The People's Party of India," he repeated slowly, pronouncing each word distinctly. "You are sure it was not the Muslim League?"

Iqbal did not catch the significance of the question.

"No, why should I be a member of the Muslim League? I . . ."

The subinspector walked out of the room before Iqbal had finished his sentence. He ordered the constables to take the prisoners to the police station. He went back to the rest house to report his discovery to the magistrate. There was an obsequious smile on his face.

"Cherisher of the poor, it is all right. He says he has been sent by the People's Party. But I am sure he is a Muslim Leaguer. They are much the same. We would have had to arrest him in any case if he was up to mischief so near the border. We can charge him with something or other later."

"How do you know he is a Muslim Leaguer?"

The subinspector smiled confidently. "I had him stripped."

Hukum Chand shook his glass to churn the dregs of chalk at the bottom, and slowly drank up the remaining portion of the seltzer. He looked thoughtfully into the empty tumbler and added:

"Fill in the warrant of arrest correctly. Name: Mohammed Iqbal, son of Mohammed Something-or-other, or just father unknown. Caste: Mussulman. Occupation: Muslim League worker."

The subinspector saluted dramatically.

"Wait, wait. Do not leave things half done. Enter in your police diary words to the effect that Ram Lal's murderers have not yet been traced but that information about them is expected soon. Didn't you say Jugga has something to do with it?"

"Yes, sir. The dacoits threw glass bangles in his courtyard before leaving. Apparently he had refused to join them in their venture."

"Well, get the names out of him quickly. Beat him if necessary."

The subinspector smiled. "I will get the names of the dacoits out of him in twenty-four hours and without any beating."

"Yes, yes, get them in any way you like," answered Hukum Chand impatiently. "Also, enter today's two arrests on separate pages of the police station diary with other items in between. Do not let there be any more bungling."

The subinspector saluted again.

"I will take good care, sir."

Iqbal and Jugga were taken to Chundunnugger police station in a tonga. Iqbal was given the place of honor in the middle of the front seat. The driver perched himself on the wooden shaft alongside the horse's flank, leaving his seat empty. Juggut Singh sat on the rear seat between two policemen. It was a long and dusty drive on an unmetaled road which ran parallel to the railway track. The only person at ease was Jugga. He knew the policemen and they knew him. Nor was the situation unfamiliar to him.

"You must have many prisoners in the police station these days," he stated.

"No, not one," answered one of the constables. "We do not arrest rioters. We only disperse them. And there is no time to deal with other crimes. Yours are the first arrests we have made in the last seven days. Both cells are vacant. You can have one all to yourself."

"Babuji will like that," Jugga said. "Won't you, Babuji?"

Iqbal did not answer. Jugga felt slightly snubbed, and tried to change the subject quickly.

"You must have a lot of work to do with this Hindustan-Pakistan business going on," he remarked to the constable.

"Yes. There is all this killing and the police force has been reduced to less than half."

"Why, have they joined up with Pakistan?"

"We do not know whether they have joined up on the other side—they kept protesting that they did not want to go at all. On the day of independence, the Superintendent Sahib disarmed all Muslim policemen and they fled. Their intentions were evil. Muslims are like that. You can never trust them."

"Yes," added another policeman, "it was the Muslim police taking sides which made the difference in the riots. Hindu boys of Lahore would have given the Muslims hell if it had not been for their police. They did a lot of *zulum*."

"Their army is like that, too. Baluch soldiers have been shooting people whenever they were sure there was no chance of running into Sikh or Gurkha troops."

"They cannot escape from God. No one can escape from God," said Juggut Singh vehemently. Everyone looked a little surprised. Even Iqbal turned round to make sure that the voice was Juggut Singh's.

"Isn't that right, Babuji? You are a clever man, you tell me, can one escape the wrath of God?"

Iqbal said nothing.

"No, of course not," Jugga answered himself. "I tell you something which Bhai Meet Singh told me. It is worth listening to, Babuji. It is absolutely sixteen annas' worth in the rupee."

Every rupee is worth sixteen annas, thought Iqbal. He refused to take interest. Jugga went on.

"The Bhai told me of a truckful of Baluch soldiers who were going from Amritsar to Lahore. When they were getting near the Pakistan border, the soldiers began to stick bayonets into Sikhs going along the road. The driver would slow down near a cyclist or a pedestrian, the soldiers on the footboard would stab him in the back and then the driver would accelerate away fast. They killed many people like this and were feeling happier and happier as they got nearer Pakistan. They were within a mile of the border and were traveling at great speed. What do you think happened then?"

"What?" asked an obliging policeman. They all listened intently—all except Iqbal. Even the driver stopped flogging the horse and looked back.

"Listen, Babuji, this is worth listening to. A pariah dog ran across the road. The very same driver of the truck who had been responsible for killing so many people swerved sharply to the right to avoid the dog, a mangy pariah dog. He crashed into a tree. The driver and two of the soldiers were killed. All the others seriously wounded. What do you say to that?"

Policemen murmured approval. Iqbal felt irritated.

"Who caused the crash, the dog or God?" he asked cynically.

"God—of course," answered one of the policemen. "Why should one who enjoyed killing human beings be bothered by a stray dog getting under his wheels?"

"You tell me," said Iqbal coldly. He squashed everyone except Jugga, who was irrepressible. Jugga turned to the tonga driver. The man had started whipping his horse again.

"Bhola, have you no fear of God that you beat your animal so mercilessly?"

Bhola stopped beating the horse. The expression on his face was resentful: it was his horse and he could do what he liked to it.

"Bholeya, how is business these days?" asked Jugga, trying to make up.

"God is merciful," answered the driver pointing to the sky with his whip, then added quickly, "Inspector Sahib is also merciful. We are alive and manage to fill our bellies."

"Don't you make money off these refugees who are wanting to go to Pakistan?"

"And lose my life for money?" asked Bhola angrily. "No, thank you, brother, you keep your advice to yourself. When the mobs attack they do not wait to find out who you are, Hindu or Muslim; they kill. The other day four Sikh Sardars in a jeep drove alongside a mile-long column of Muslim refugees walking on the road. Without warning they opened fire with their sten guns. Four sten guns! God alone knows how many they killed. What would happen if a mob got hold of my tonga full of Muslims? They would kill me first and ask afterwards."

"Why didn't a dog get under the jeep and upset it?" asked Iqbal sarcastically.

There was an awkward pause. No one knew what to say to this sour-tempered babu. Jugga asked naively:

"Babuji, don't you believe that bad acts yield a bitter harvest? It is the law of karma. So the bhai is always saying. The Guru has also said the same in the Book."

"Yes, absolutely, sixteen annas in the rupee," sneered Iqbal.

"Achaji, have it your own way," said Jugga, still smiling. "You will never agree with ordinary people." He turned to the driver again.

"Bholeya, I hear a lot of women are being abducted and sold cheap. You could find a wife for yourself."

"Why, Sardara, if you can find a Mussulmani without paying

for her, am I impotent that I should have to buy an abducted woman?" replied Bhola.

Jugga was taken aback. His temper began to rise. The policemen, who had started to snigger, looked nervously at Juggut Singh. Bhola regretted his mistake.

"Why, Juggia," he said, changing his tone. "You make fun of others, but get angry when someone retorts."

"If these handcuffs and fetters had not been on me, I would have broken every bone in your body," said Jugga fiercely. "You are lucky to have escaped today, but if I hear you repeat this thing again I will tear your tongue out of your mouth." Jugga spat loudly.

Bhola was thoroughly frightened. "Do not lose your temper. What have I . . . "

"Bastard."

That was the end of the conversation. The uneasy silence in the tonga was broken only by Bhola swearing at his horse. Jugga was lost in angry thoughts. He was surprised that his clandestine meetings were public knowledge. Somebody had probably seen him and Nooran talking to each other. That must have started the gossip. If a tonga driver from Chundunnugger knew, everyone in Mano Majra would have been talking about it for some time. The last to learn gossip are the parties concerned. Perhaps Imam Baksh and his daughter Nooran were the only ones in the village who knew nothing of what was being said.

The party reached Chundunnugger after noon. The tonga came to a halt outside the police station, which was a couple of furlongs distant from the town. The prisoners were escorted through an arched gateway which had WELCOME painted on it in large letters. They were first taken to the reporting room. The head constable opened a large register and made the entries of the day's events on separate pages. Just above the table was an old framed picture of King George VI with a placard stating in Urdu, BRIBERY IS A CRIME. On another wall was pasted a colored portrait of Gandhi torn from a calendar. Beneath it was a motto written in English, HONESTY IS THE BEST POLICY. Other portraits in the room were those of absconders, bad characters, and missing persons.

After the daily diary entries had been made, the prisoners were taken across the courtyard to their cells. There were only two cells in the police station. These were on one side of the courtyard facing the policemen's barracks. The wall of the farther end of the square was covered by railway creeper.

Jugga's arrival was the subject of much hilarity.

"Oye, you are back again. You think it is your father-in-law's house," shouted one of the constables from his barrack.

"It is, seeing the number of policemen's daughters I have seduced," answered Juggut Singh at the top of his voice. He had forgotten the unpleasantness in the tonga.

"Oye, Budmasha, you will not desist from your budmashi. Wait till the Inspector Sahib hears of what you said and he will put hot chillies up your bottom."

"You cannot do that to your son-in-law!"

With Iqbal it was different. His handcuffs were removed with apologies, A chair, a table, and a charpoy were put in his cell. The head constable collected all the daily newspapers and magazines, English and Urdu, that he could find and left them in the cell. Iqbal's food was served on a brass plate and a small pitcher and a glass tumbler were put on the table beside his charpoy. Jugga was given no furniture in his cell. His food was literally flung at him and he ate his chapatties out of his hand. A constable poured water onto his cupped palm through the iron bars. Jugga's bed was the hard cement floor.

The difference in treatment did not surprise Iqbal. In a country which had accepted caste distinctions for many centuries, inequality had become an inborn mental concept. If caste was abolished by legislation, it came up in other forms of class distinction. In thoroughly westernized circles like that of the civil servants in the government secretariat in Delhi, places for parking cars were marked according to seniority, and certain entrances to offices were reserved for higher officials. Lavatories were graded according to rank and labeled SENIOR OFFICERS, JUNIOR OFFICERS, CLERKS AND STENOGRAPHERS and OTHER RANKS. With a mental make-up so thoroughly sectionalized, grading according to their social status people who were charged or convicted of the same offence did not appear incongruous. Iqbal was A-class. Jugga was the rock-bottom C.

After his midday meal, Iqbal lay down on the charpoy. He heard snoring from Jugga's cell. But he himself was far too disturbed to sleep. His mind was like the delicate spring of a watch, which quivers for several hours after it has been touched. He sat up and began to turn over the pile of newspapers the head constable had left him. They were all alike: the same news, the same statements, the same editorials. Except for the wording of the headlines, they might all have been written by the same hand. Even the photographs were the same. In disgust, he turned to the matrimonial ads. There was sometimes entertainment there. But the youth of the Punjab were as alike as the news. The qualities they required in a wife were identical. All wanted virgins. A few, more broad-minded than the rest, were willing to consider widows, but only if they had not been deflowered. All demanded women who were good at h. h. a., or household affairs. To the advanced and charitable, c. & d. [caste and dowry] were no bar. Not many asked for photographs of their prospective wives. Beauty, they recognized, was only skin-deep. Most wanted to "correspond with horoscopes." Astronomical harmony was the one guarantee of happiness. Iqbal threw the papers away, and rummaged through the magazines. If anything, they were worse than the newspapers. There was the inevitable article on the Ajanta cave frescoes. There was the article on Indian ballet. There was the article on Tagore. There was the article on the stories of Prem Chand. There were the articles on the private lives of film stars. Iqbal gave up, and lay down again. He felt depressed about everything. It occurred to him that he had hardly slept for three days. He wondered if this would be considered a "sacrifice." It was possible. He must find some way of sending word to the party. Then, perhaps . . . He fell asleep with visions of banner headlines announcing his arrest, his release, his triumphant emergence as a leader.

In the evening a policeman came to Iqbal's cell, carrying another chair.

"Is somebody going to share my cell?" asked Iqbal a little apprehensively.

"No, Babuji. Only the Inspector Sahib. He wishes to have a word with you. He is coming now."

Iqbal did not answer. The policeman studied the position of the chair for a moment. Then he withdrew. There was a sound of voices in the corridor, and the subinspector appeared.

"Have I your permission to enter?"

Iqbal nodded. "What can I do for you, Inspector Sahib?"

"We are your slaves, Mr. Iqbal. You should command us and we will serve you," the subinspector answered with a smile. He was proud of his ability to change his tone and manner as the circumstances required. That was diplomacy.

"I did not know you were so kind to people you arrested for murder. It is on a charge of murder that you have brought me here, isn't it? I do not suppose your policemen told you I came to Mano Majra yesterday on the same train as they did."

"We have framed no charge. That is for the court. We are only detaining you on suspicion. We cannot allow political agitators in the border areas." The subinspector continued to smile. "Why don't you go and do your propaganda in Pakistan where you belong?"

Iqbal was stung to fury, but he tried to suppress any sign of his anger.

"What exactly do you mean by 'belonging to Pakistan,' Inspector Sahib?"

"You are a Muslim. You go to Pakistan."

"That is a bloody lie," exploded Iqbal. "What is more, you know it is a bloody lie. You just want to cover up your stupidity by trumping up a false case."

The subinspector spoke back sourly.

"You should use your tongue with some discrimination, Mr. Iqbal. I am not in your father's pay to have to put up with your 'bloody's.' Your name is Iqbal and you are circumcised. I have examined you myself. Also, you cannot give any explanation for your presence in Mano Majra. That is enough."

"It will not be enough when it comes up in court, and in the newspapers. I am not a Muslim—not that that matters—and what I came to Mano Majra for is none of your business. If you do not release me within twenty-four hours I will move a habeas corpus petition and tell the court the way you go about your duties."

"Habeas corpus petition?" The subinspector roared with laughter. "It seems you have been living in foreign lands too long, Mr. Iqbal. Even now you live in a fool's paradise. You will live and learn."

The subinspector left the cell abruptly, and locked the steel bar gate. He opened the adjoining one behind which Jugga was locked.

"Sat Sri Akal, Inspector Sahib."

The subinspector did not acknowledge the greeting.

"Will you ever give up being a budmash?"

"King of pearls, you can say what you like, but this time I am innocent. I swear by the Guru I am innocent."

Jugga remained seated on the floor. The subinspector stood leaning against the wall.

"Where were you on the night of the dacoity?"

"I had nothing to do with the dacoity," answered Jugga evasively.

"Where were you on the night of the dacoity?" repeated the subinspector.

Jugga looked down at the floor. "I had gone to my fields. It was my turn of water."

The subinspector knew he was lying. "I can check up the turn of water with the canal man. Did you inform the lambardar that you were going out of the village?"

Jugga only shuffled his feet and kept on looking at the floor.

"Your mother said you had gone to drive away wild pigs."

Jugga continued to shuffle his feet. After a long pause he said again, "I had nothing to do with the dacoity. I am innocent."

"Who were the dacoits?"

"King of pearls, how should I know who the dacoits were? I was out of the village at the time, otherwise you think anyone would have dared to rob and kill in Mano Majra?"

"Who were the dacoits?" repeated the subinspector menacingly. "I know you know them. They certainly know you. They left a gift of glass bangles for you."

Jugga did not reply.

"You want to be whipped on your buttocks or have red chillies put up your rectum before you talk?"

Jugga winced. He knew what the subinspector meant. He had been through it—once. Hands and feet pinned under legs of charpoys with half a dozen policemen sitting on them. Testicles twisted and squeezed till one became senseless with pain. Powdered red chillies thrust up the rectum by rough hands, and the sensation of having the tail on fire for several days. All this, and no food or water, or hot spicy food with a bowl of shimmering cool water put outside the cell just beyond one's reach. The memory shook him.

"No," he said. "For God's sake, no." He flung himself on the floor and clasped the subinspector's shoes with both his hands. "Please, O king of pearls." He was ashamed of himself, but he knew he could never endure such torture again. "I am innocent. By the name of the Guru, I had nothing to do with the dacoity."

Seeing six foot four of muscle cringing at his feet gave the subinspector a feeling of elation. He had never known anyone to hold out against physical pain, not one. The pattern of torture had to be carefully chosen. Some succumbed to hunger, others—of the Iqbal type—to the inconvenience of having to defecate in front of the policemen. Some to flies sitting on their faces smeared with treacle, with their hands tied behind them. Some to lack of sleep. In the end they all gave in.

"I will give you two days to tell me the names of the dacoits," he said. "Otherwise, I will beat your behind till it looks like the tail of a ram."

The subinspector freed his feet from Jugga's hands and walked out. His visits had been a failure. He would have to change his tactics. It was frustrating to deal with two people so utterly different.

KALYUG

ARLY in September the time schedule in Mano Majra started going wrong. Trains became less punctual than ever before and many more started to run through at night. Some days it seemed as though the alarm clock had been set for the wrong hour. On others, it was as if no one had remembered to wind it. Imam Baksh waited for Meet Singh to make the first start. Meet Singh waited for the mullah's call to prayer before getting up. People stayed in bed late without realizing that times had changed and the mail train might not run through at all. Children did not know when to be hungry, and clamored for food all the time. In the evenings, everyone was indoors before sunset and in bed before the express came by—if it did come by. Goods trains had stopped running altogether, so there was no lullaby to lull them to sleep. Instead, ghost trains went past at odd hours between midnight and dawn, disturbing the dreams of Mano Majra.

This was not all that changed the life of the village. A unit of Sikh soldiers arrived and put up tents near the railway station. They built a six-foot-high square of sandbags about the base of the signal near the bridge, and mounted a machine gun in each face. Armed sentries began to patrol the platform and no villagers were allowed near the railings. All trains coming from Delhi stopped and changed their drivers and guards before moving on to Pakistan. Those coming from Pakistan ran through with their engines screaming with release and relief.

One morning, a train from Pakistan halted at Mano Majra railway station. At first glance, it had the look of the trains in the days of peace. No one sat on the roof. No one clung between the bogies. No one was balanced on the footboards. But some-how it was different. There was something uneasy about it. It had a ghostly quality. As soon as it pulled up to the platform, the guard emerged from the tail end of the train and went into the stationmaster's office. Then the two went to the soldiers' tents and spoke to the officer in charge. The soldiers were called out and the villagers loitering about were ordered back to Mano Majra. One man was sent off on a motorcycle to Chundunnugger. An hour later, the subinspector with about fifty armed policemen turned up at the station. Immediately after them, Mr. Hukum Chand drove up in his American car.

The arrival of the ghost train in broad daylight created a commotion in Mano Majra. People stood on their roofs to see what was happening at the station. All they could see was the black top of the train stretching from one end of the platform to the other. The station building and the railings blocked the rest of the train from view. Occasionally a soldier or a police-man came out of the station and then went back again.

In the afternoon, men gathered in little groups, discussing the train. The groups merged with each other under the peepul tree, and then everyone went into the gurdwara. Women, who had gone from door to door collecting and dropping bits of gossip, assembled in the headman's house and waited for their menfolk to come home and tell them what they had learned about the train.

This was the pattern of things at Mano Majra when anything of consequence happened. The women went to the headman's house, the men to the temple. There was no recognized leader of the village. Banta Singh, the headman, was really only a col-lector of revenue—a lambardar. The post had been in his family for several generations. He did not own any more land than the others. Nor was he a head in any other way. He had no airs about him: he was a modest hard-working peasant like the rest of his fellow villagers. But since government officials and the police dealt with him, he had an official status. Nobody called him by his name. He was "O Lambardara," as his father, his father's father, and his father's father's father had been before him.

The only men who voiced their opinions at village meetings were Imam Baksh, the mullah of the mosque, and Bhai Meet Singh. Imam Baksh was a weaver, and weavers are traditionally the butts of jokes in the Punjab. They are considered effeminate and cowardly—a race of cuckolds whose women are always having liaisons with others. But Imam Baksh's age and piety had made him respected. A series of tragedies in his family had made him an object of pity, and then of affection. The Punjabis love people they can pity. His wife and only son had died within a few days of each other. His eyes, which had never been very good, suddenly became worse and he could not work his looms any more. He was reduced to beggary, with a baby girl, Nooran, to look after. He began living in the mosque and teaching Muslim children the Koran. He wrote out verses from the Koran for the village folk to wear as charms or for the sick to swallow as medicine. Small offerings of flour, vegetables, food, and castoff clothes kept him and his daughter alive. He had an amazing fund of anecdotes and proverbs which the peasants loved to hear. His appearance commanded respect. He was a tall, lean man, bald save for a line of white hair which ran round the back of his head from ear to ear, and he had a neatly trimmed silky white beard that he occasionally dyed with henna to a deep orange-red. The cataract in his eyes gave them a misty philosophical look. Despite his sixty years, he held himself erect. All this gave his bearing a dignity and an aura of righteousness. He was known to the villagers not as Imam Baksh or the mullah but as *chacha*, or "Uncle."

Meet Singh inspired no such affection and respect. He was only a peasant who had taken to religion as an escape from work. He had a little land of his own which he had leased out, and this, with the offerings at the temple, gave him a comfortable living. He had no wife or children. He was not learned

79

in the scriptures, nor had he any faculty for conversation. Even his appearance was against him. He was short, fat, and hairy. He was the same age as Imam Baksh, but his beard had none of the serenity of the other's. It was black, with streaks of gray. And he was untidy. He wore his turban only when reading the scripture. Otherwise, he went about with his long hair tied in a loose knot held by a little wooden comb. Almost half of the hair was scattered on the nape of his neck. He seldom wore a shirt and his only garment—a pair of shorts—was always greasy with dirt. But Meet Singh was a man of peace. Envy had never poisoned his affection for Imam Baksh. He only felt that he owed it to his own community to say something when Imam Baksh made any suggestions. Their conversation always had an undercurrent of friendly rivalry.

The meeting in the gurdwara had a melancholic atmosphere. People had little to say, and those who did spoke slowly, like prophets.

Imam Baksh opened the discussion. "May Allah be merciful. We are living in bad times."

A few people sighed solemnly, "Yes, bad days."

Meet Singh added, "Yes, Chacha—this is Kalyug, the dark age."

There was a long silence and people shuffled uneasily on their haunches. Some yawned, closing their mouths with loud invocations to God: "Ya Allah. Wah Guru, wah Guru."

"Lambardara," started Imam Baksh again, "you should know what is happening. Why has not the Deputy Sahib sent for you?"

"How am I to know, Chacha? When he sends for me I will go. He is also at the station and no one is allowed near it."

A young villager interjected in a loud cheery voice: "We are not going to die just yet. We will soon know what is going on. It is a train after all. It may be carrying government treasures or arms. So they guard it. Haven't you heard, many have been looted?"

"Shut up," rebuked his bearded father angrily. "Where there are elders, what need have you to talk?"

"I only . . . "

"That is all," said the father sternly. No one spoke for some time.

"I have heard," said Imam Baksh, slowly combing his beard with his fingers, "that there have been many incidents with trains."

The word "incident" aroused an uneasy feeling in the audience. "Yes, lots of incidents have been heard of," Meet Singh agreed after a while.

"We only ask for Allah's mercy," said Imam Baksh, closing the subject he had himself opened.

Meet Singh, not meaning to be outdone in the invocation to God, added, "Wah Guru, wah Guru."

They sat on in a silence punctuated by yawns and murmurs of "Ya Allah" and "Hey wah Guru." Several people, on the outer fringe of the assembly, stretched themselves on the floor and went to sleep.

Suddenly a policeman appeared in the doorway of the gurdwara. The lambardar and three or four villagers stood up. People who were asleep were prodded into getting up. Those who had been dozing sat up in a daze, exclaiming, "What is it? What's up?" Then hurriedly wrapped their turbans round their heads.

"Who is the lambardar of the village?"

Banta Singh walked up to the door. The policeman took him aside and whispered something. Then as Banta Singh turned back, he said loudly: "Quickly, within half an hour. There are two military trucks waiting on the station side. I will be there."

The policeman walked away briskly.

The villagers crowded round Banta Singh. The possession of a secret had lent him an air of importance. His voice had a tone of authority.

"Everyone get all the wood there is in his house and all the kerosene oil he can spare and bring these to the motor trucks on the station side. You will be paid."

The villagers waited for him to tell them why. He ordered them off brusquely. "Are you deaf? Haven't you heard? Or do you want the police to whip your buttocks before you move? Come along quickly."

People dispersed into the village lanes whispering to each other. The lambardar went to his own house.

A few minutes later, villagers with bundles of wood and bottles of oil started assembling outside the village on the station side. Two large mud-green army trucks were parked alongside each other. A row of empty petrol cans stood against a mud wall. A Sikh soldier with a sten gun stood on guard. Another Sikh, an officer with his beard neatly rolled in a hair net, sat on the back of one of the trucks with his feet dangling. He watched the wood being stacked in the other truck and nodded his head in reply to the villagers' greetings. The lambardar stood beside him, taking down the names of the villagers and the quantities they brought. After dumping their bundles of wood on the truck and emptying bottles of kerosene into the petrol cans, the villagers collected in a little group at a respectful distance from the officer.

Imam Baksh put down on the truck the wood he had carried on his head and handed his bottle of oil to the lambardar. He re-tied his turban, then greeted the officer loudly, "Salaam, Sardar Sahib."

The officer looked away.

Imam Baksh started again, "Everything is all right, isn't it, Sardar Sahib?"

The officer turned around abruptly and snapped, "Get along. Don't you see I am busy?"

Imam Baksh, still adjusting his turban, meekly joined the villagers.

When both the trucks were loaded, the officer told Banta

Singh to come to the camp next morning for the money. The trucks rumbled off toward the station.

Banta Singh was surrounded by eager villagers. He felt that he was somehow responsible for the insult to Imam Baksh. The villagers were impatient with him.

"O Lambardara, who don't you tell us something? What is all this big secret you are carrying about? You seem to think you have become someone very important and don't need to talk to us any more," said Meet Singh angrily.

"No, Bhai, no. If I knew, why would I not tell you? You talk like children. How can I argue with soldiers and policemen? They told me nothing. And didn't you see how that pig's penis spoke to Chacha? One's self-respect is in one's own hands. Why should I have myself insulted by having my turban taken off?"

Imam Baksh acknowledged the gesture gracefully. "Lambardar is right. If somebody barks when you speak to him, it is best to keep quiet. Let us all go to our homes. You can see what they are doing from the tops of your roofs."

The villagers dispersed to their rooftops. From there the trucks could be seen at the camp near the station. They started off again and went east along the railway track till they were beyond the signal. Then they turned sharp left and bumped across the rails. They turned left again, came back along the line toward the station, and disappeared behind the train.

All afternoon, the villagers stood on their roofs shouting to each other, asking whether anyone had seen anything. In their excitement they had forgotten to prepare the midday meal. Mothers fed their children on stale leftovers from the day before. They did not have time to light their hearths. The men did not give fodder to their cattle nor remember to milk them as evening drew near. When the sun was already under the arches of the bridge everyone became conscious of having overlooked the daily chores. It would be dark soon and the children would clamor for food, but still the women watched, their eyes glued to the station. The cows and buffaloes lowed in the barns, but still the men stayed on the roofs looking toward the station. Everyone expected something to happen.

The sun sank behind the bridge, lighting the white clouds which had appeared in the sky with hues of russet, copper, and orange. Then shades of gray blended with the glow as evening gave way to twilight and twilight sank into darkness. The station became a black wall. Wearily, the men and women went down to their courtyards, beckoning the others to do the same. They did not want to be alone in missing anything.

The northern horizon, which had turned a bluish gray, showed orange again. The orange turned into copper and then into a luminous russet. Red tongues of flame leaped into the black sky. A soft breeze began to blow toward the village. It brought the smell of burning kerosene, then of wood. And then—a faint acrid smell of searing flesh.

The village was stilled in a deathly silence. No one asked anyone else what the odor was. They all knew. They had known it all the time. The answer was implicit in the fact that the train had come from Pakistan.

That evening, for the first time in the memory of Mano Majra, Imam Baksh's sonorous cry did not rise to the heavens to proclaim the glory of God.

The day's happenings cast their gloom on the rest house. Mr. Hukum Chand had been out since the morning. When his orderly came from the station at midday for a thermos flask of tea and sandwiches, he told the bearer and the sweeper about the train. In the evening, the servants and their families saw the flames shooting up above the line of trees. The fire cast a melancholy amber light on the khaki walls of the bungalow.

The day's work had taken a lot out of Hukum Chand. His fatigue was not physical. The sight of so many dead had at first produced a cold numbness. Within a couple of hours, all his emotions were dead, and he watched corpses of men and women

84

and children being dragged out, with as little interest as if they had been trunks or bedding. But by evening, he began to feel forlorn and sorry for himself. He looked weary and haggard when he stepped out of the car. The bearer, the sweeper, and their families were on the roof looking at the flames. He had to wait for them to come down and open the doors. His bath had not been drawn. Hukum Chand felt neglected and more depressed. He lay on his bed, ignoring the servants' attentions. One unlaced and took off his shoes and began to rub his feet. The other brought in buckets of water and filled the bathtub. The magistrate got up abruptly, almost kicking the servant, and went into the bathroom.

After a bath and a change of clothes, Hukum Chand felt somewhat refreshed. The punkah breeze was cool and soothing. He lay down again with his hands over his eyes. Within the dark chambers of his closed eyes, scenes of the day started coming back in panoramic succession. He tried to squash them by pressing his fingers into his eyes. The images only went blacker and redder and then came back. There was a man holding his intestines, with an expression in his eyes which said: "Look what I have got!" There were women and children huddled in a corner, their eyes dilated with horror, their mouths still open as if their shrieks had just then become voiceless. Some of them did not have a scratch on their bodies. There were bodies crammed against the far end wall of the compartment, looking in terror at the empty windows through which must have come shots, spears and spikes. There were lavatories jammed with corpses of young men who had muscled their way to comparative safety. And all the nauseating smell of putrefying flesh, feces and urine. The very thought made vomit come up in Hukum Chand's mouth. The most vivid picture was that of an old peasant with a long white beard; he did not look dead at all. He sat jammed between rolls of bedding on the upper rack meant for luggage, looking pensively at the scene below him. A thin crimson line of coagulated blood ran from his ear onto his beard.

Hukum Chand had shaken him by the shoulder, saying "Baba, Baba!" believing he was alive. He was alive. His cold hand stretched itself grotesquely and gripped the magistrate's right foot. Cold sweat came out all over Hukum Chand's body. He tried to shout but could only open his mouth. The hand moved up slowly from the ankles to the calf, from the calf to the knee, gripping its way all along. Hukum Chand tried to shout again. His voice stuck in his throat. The hand kept moving upwards. As it touched the fleshy part of his thigh, its grip loosened. Hukum Chand began to moan and then with a final effort broke out of the nightmare with an agonized shriek. He sat up with a look of terror in his eyes.

The bearer was standing beside him looking equally frightened.

"I thought the Sahib was tired and would like his feet pressed."

Hukum Chand could not speak. He wiped the sweat off his forehead and sank back on the pillow, exclaiming "Hai Ram, hai Ram." The nervous outburst purged him of fear. He felt weak and foolish. After some time a sense of calm descended on him.

"Get me some whisky."

The bearer brought him a tray with whisky, soda, and a tumbler. Hukum Chand filled a quarter of the glass with the honey-colored liquid. The bearer filled the rest with soda. The magistrate drank half of the glass in a gulp and lay back. The alcohol poured into his system, warming his jaded nerves to life. The servant started pressing his feet again. He looked up at the ceiling, feeling relaxed and just pleasantly tired. The sweeper started lighting lamps in the rooms. He put one on the table beside Hukum Chand's bed. A moth fluttered round the chimney and flew up in spirals to the ceiling. The geckos darted across from the wall. The moth hit the ceiling well out of the geckos' reach and spiraled back to the lamp. The lizards watched with their shining black eyes. The moth flew up again and down again. Hukum Chand knew that if it alighted on the ceiling for a second, one of the geckos would get it fluttering between its little crocodile jaws. Perhaps that was its destiny. It was everyone's destiny. Whether it was in hospitals, trains, or in the jaws of reptiles, it was all the same. One could even die in bed alone and no one would discover until the stench spread all round and maggots moved in and out of the sockets of the eyes and geckos ran over the face with their slimy clammy bellies. Hukum Chand wiped his face with his hands. How could one escape one's own mind! He gulped the rest of the whisky and poured himself another.

Death had always been an obsession with Hukum Chand. As a child, he had seen his aunt die after the birth of a dead child. Her whole system had been poisoned. For days she had hallucinations and had waved her arms about frantically to ward off the spirit of death which stood at the foot of her bed. She had died shrieking with terror, staring and pointing at the wall. The scene had never left Hukum Chand's mind. Later in his youth, he had fought the fear of death by spending many hours at a cremation ground near the university. He had watched young and old brought on crude bamboo stretchers, lamented for, and then burned. Visits to the cremation ground left him with a sense of tranquillity. He had got over the immediate terror of death, but the idea of ultimate dissolution was always present in his mind. It made him kind, charitable and tolerant. It even made him cheerful in adversity. He had taken the loss of his children with phlegmatic resignation. He had borne with an illiterate, unattractive wife, without complaint. It all came from his belief that the only absolute truth was death. The rest—love, ambition, pride, values of all kinds—was to be taken with a pinch of salt. He did so with a clear conscience. Although he accepted gifts and obliged friends when they got into trouble, he was not corrupt. He occasionally joined in parties, arranged for singing and dancing—and sometimes sex—but he was not immoral. What did it really matter in the end? That was the core of Hukum Chand's philosophy of life, and he lived well.

But a trainload of dead was too much for even Hukum Chand's fatalism. He could not square a massacre with a philosophical belief in the inevitability of death. It bewildered and frightened him by its violence and its magnitude. The picture of his aunt biting her tongue and bleeding at the mouth, her eyes staring at space, came back to him in all its vivid horror. Whisky did not help to take it away.

The room was lit by the headlights of the car and then left darker than before; the car had probably been put into the garage. Hukum Chand grew conscious of the coming night. The servants would soon be retiring to their quarters to sleep snugly surrounded by their women and children. He would be left alone in the bungalow with its empty rooms peopled by phantoms of his own creation. No! No! He must get the orderlies to sleep somewhere nearby. On the verandah perhaps? Or would they suspect he was scared? He would tell them that he might be wanted during the night and must have them at hand; that would pass unnoticed.

"Bairah."

"Sahib." The bearer came in through the wire gauze door.

"Where have you put my charpoy for the night?"

"Sahib's bed has not been laid yet. It is clouded and there might be rain. Would Huzoor like to sleep on the verandah?"

"No, I will stay in my room. The boy can pull the punkah for an hour or two till it gets cool. Tell the orderlies to sleep on the verandah. I may want them for urgent work tonight," he added, without looking up at the man.

"Yes, Sahib. I will tell them straightaway before they go to bed. Should I bring the Sahib's dinner?"

Hukum Chand had forgotten about dinner.

"No, I do not want any dinner. Just tell the orderlies to put their beds on the verandah. Tell the driver to be there too. If there is not enough space on the verandah, tell him to sleep in the next room."

The bearer went out. Hukum Chand felt relieved. He had

saved face. He could sleep peacefully with all these people about him. He listened to the reassuring sounds of human activity— the servants arguing about places on the verandah, beds being laid just outside his door, a lamp being brought in the next room, and furniture being moved to make place for charpoys.

The headlights of the car coming in lit the room once more. The car stopped outside the verandah. Hukum Chand heard voices of men and women, then the jingle of bells. He sat up and looked through the wire gauze door. It was the party of musicians, the old woman and the girl prostitute. He had forgotten about them.

"Bairah."

"Huzoor."

"Tell the driver to take the musicians and the old woman back. And . . . let the servants sleep in their quarters. If I need them, I will send for them."

Hukum Chand felt a little stupid being caught like that. The servants would certainly laugh about it. But he did not care. He poured himself another whisky.

The servants started moving out before the bearer came to speak to them. The lamp in the next room was removed. The driver started the car again. He switched on the headlights and switched them off again. The old woman would not get in the car and began to argue with the bearer. Her voice rose higher and higher till it passed the bounds of argument and addressed itself to the magistrate inside the room.

"May your government go on forever. May your pen inscribe figures of thousands—nay, hundreds of thousands."

Hukum Chand lost his temper. "Go!" he shouted. "You have to pay my debt of the other day. Go! Bearer, send her away!"

The woman's voice came down. She was quickly hustled into the car. The car went out, leaving only the flickering yellow light of the oil lamp beside Hukum Chand's bed. He rose, picked up the lamp and the table, and put them in the corner by the door. The moth circled round the glass chimney, hitting the wall on either side. The geckos crawled down from the ceiling to the wall near the lamp. As the moth alighted on the wall, one of the geckos crept up stealthily behind it, pounced, and caught it fluttering in its jaws. Hukum Chand watched the whole thing with bland indifference.

The door opened and shut gently. A small dark figure slid into the room. The silver sequins on the girl's sari twinkled in the lamplight and sent a hundred spots of light playing on the walls and the ceiling. Hukum Chand turned around. The girl stood staring at him with her large black eyes. The diamond in her nose glittered brightly. She looked thoroughly frightened.

"Come," said the magistrate, making room for her beside him and holding out his hand.

The girl came and sat down on the edge of the bed, looking away. Hukum Chand put his arm round her waist. He stroked her thighs and belly and played with her little unformed breasts. She sat impassive and rigid. Hukum Chand shuffled further away and mumbled drowsily, "Come and lie down." The girl stretched herself beside the magistrate. The sequins on her sari tickled his face. She wore perfume made of *khas;* it had the fresh odor of dry earth when water has been sprinkled on it. Her breath smelled of cardamom, her bosom of honey. Hukum Chand snuggled against her like a child and fell fast asleep.

Monsoon is not another word for rain. As its original Arabic name indicates, it is a season. There is a summer monsoon as well as a winter monsoon, but it is only the nimbose southwest winds of summer that make a *mausem*—the season of the rains. The winter monsoon is simply rain in winter. It is like a cold shower on a frosty morning. It leaves one chilled and shivering. Although it is good for the crops, people pray for it to end. Fortunately, it does not last very long.

The summer monsoon is quite another affair. It is preceded

by several months of working up a thirst so that when the waters come they are drunk deep and with relish. From the end of February, the sun starts getting hotter and spring gives way to summer. Flowers wither. Then flowering trees take their place. First come the orange showers of the flame of the forest, the vermilion of the coral tree, and the virginal white of the champac. They are followed by the mauve Jacaranda, the flamboyant gol mohur, and the soft gold cascades of the laburnum. Then the trees also lose their flowers. Their leaves fall. Their bare branches stretch up to the sky begging for water, but there is no water. The sun comes up earlier than before and licks up the drops of dew before the fevered earth can moisten its lips. It blazes away all day long in a cloudless gray sky, drying up wells, streams and lakes. It sears the grass and thorny scrub till they catch fire. The fires spread and dry jungles burn like matchwood.

The sun goes on, day after day, from east to west, scorching relentlessly. The earth cracks up and deep fissures open their gaping mouths asking for water; but there is no water—only the shimmering haze at noon making mirage lakes of quicksilver. Poor villagers take their thirsty cattle out to drink and are struck dead. The rich wear sunglasses and hide behind chicks of khus fiber on which their servants pour water.

The sun makes an ally of the breeze. It heats the air till it becomes the loo and then sends it on its errand. Even in the intense heat, the loo's warm caresses are sensuous and pleasant. It brings up the prickly heat. It produces a numbness which makes the head nod and the eyes heavy with sleep. It brings on a stroke which takes its victim as gently as breeze bears a fluff of thistledown.

Then comes a period of false hopes. The loo drops. The air becomes still. From the southern horizon a black wall begins to advance. Hundreds of kites and crows fly ahead. Can it be . . . ? No, it is a dust storm. A fine powder begins to fall. A solid mass of locusts covers the sun. They devour whatever is left on the trees and in the fields. Then comes the storm itself. In furious sweeps it smacks open doors and windows, banging them forward and backward, smashing their glass panes. Thatched roofs and corrugated iron sheets are borne aloft into the sky like bits of paper. Trees are torn up by the roots and fall across power lines. The tangled wires electrocute people and start fires in houses. The storm carries the flames to other houses till there is a conflagration. All this happens in a few seconds. Before you can say *Chakravartyrajagopalachari*, the gale is gone. The dust hanging in the air settles on your books, furniture and food; it gets in your eyes and ears and throat and nose.

This happens over and over again until the people have lost all hope. They are disillusioned, dejected, thirsty and sweating. The prickly heat on the back of their necks is like emery paper. There is another lull. A hot petrified silence prevails. Then comes the shrill, strange call of a bird. Why has it left its cool bosky shade and come out in the sun? People look up wearily at the lifeless sky. Yes, there it is with its mate! They are like large black-and-white bulbuls with perky crests and long tails. They are pie-crested cuckoos who have flown all the way from Africa ahead of the monsoon. Isn't there a gentle breeze blowing? And hasn't it a damp smell? And wasn't the rumble which drowned the birds' anguished cry the sound of thunder? The people hurry to the roofs to see. The same ebony wall is coming up from the east. A flock of herons fly across. There is a flash of lightning which outshines the daylight. The wind fills the black sails of the clouds and they billow out across the sun. A profound shadow falls on the earth. There is another clap of thunder. Big drops of rain fall and dry up in the dust. A fragrant smell rises from the earth. Another flash of lightning and another crack of thunder like the roar of a hungry tiger. It has come! Sheets of water, wave after wave. The people lift their faces to the clouds and let the abundance of water cover them. Schools and offices close. All work stops. Men, women, and children run madly about the streets, waving their arms and shouting "Ho, Ho,"—hosannas to the miracle of the monsoon.

The monsoon is not like ordinary rain which comes and goes. Once it is on, it stays for two months or more. Its advent is greeted with joy. Parties set out for picnics and litter the countryside with the skins and stones of mangoes. Women and children make swings on branches of trees and spend the day in sport and song. Peacocks spread their tails and strut about with their mates; the woods echo with their shrill cries.

But after a few days the flush of enthusiasm is gone. The earth becomes a big stretch of swamp and mud. Wells and lakes fill up and burst their bounds. In towns, gutters get clogged and streets become turbid streams. In villages, mud walls of huts melt in the water and thatched roofs sag and descend on the inmates. Rivers which keep rising steadily from the time the summer's heat starts melting the snows, suddenly turn to floods as the monsoon spends itself on the mountains. Roads, railway tracks and bridges go under water. Houses near the riverbanks are swept down to the sea.

With the monsoon, the tempo of life and death increases. Almost overnight grass begins to grow and leafless trees turn green. Snakes, centipedes and scorpions are born out of nothing. The ground is strewn with earthworms, ladybirds and tiny frogs. At night, myriads of moths flutter around the lamps. They fall in everybody's food and water. Geckos dart about filling themselves with insects till they get heavy and fall off ceilings. Inside rooms the hum of mosquitoes is maddening. People spray clouds of insecticide, and the floor becomes a layer of wriggling bodies and wings. Next evening, there are many more fluttering around the lamp shades and burning themselves in the flames.

While the monsoon lasts, the showers start and stop without warning. The clouds fly across, dropping their rain on the plains as it pleases them, till they reach the Himalayas. They climb up the mountainsides. Then the cold squeezes the last drops of water out of them. Lightning and thunder never cease. All this happens in late August or early September. Then the season of the rains gives way to autumn.

A roll of thunder woke Hukum Chand. He opened his eyes. There was a gray light in the room. In the corner, a weary yellow flame flickered through the soot of the lamp chimney. There was a flash of lightning followed by another peal of thunder. A gust of cool, damp breeze blew across the room. The lamp fluttered and went out. Raindrops began to fall in a gentle patter.

Rain! At long last the rain, thought the magistrate. The monsoon had been a poor one. Clouds had come, but they were high and fleecy and floated by, leaving the land thirstier than before. September was very late for the rain, but that only made it more welcome. It smelled good, it sounded good, it looked good— and above all, it did good. Ah, but did it? Hukum Chand felt feverish. The corpses! A thousand charred corpses sizzling and smoking while the rain put out the fire. A hundred yards of charred corpses! Beads of sweat broke out on his temples. He felt cold and frightened. He reached across the bed. The girl had left. He was all alone in the bungalow. He got his wrist watch from under the pillow and cupped his hands round the dial. The glow-worm green of the radium hands pointed to 6:30. He felt comforted. It was fairly late in the morning. The sky must be heavily overcast. Then he heard the sound of coughing on the verandah, and felt reassured. He sat up with a jerk.

A dull pain rocked his forehead. He shut his eyes and held his head between his hands. The throbbing ebbed away. He had drunk too much whisky and had eaten nothing. After a few minutes, he opened his eyes, looked around the room—and saw the girl. She hadn't left. She was asleep on the big cane armchair, wrapped in her black sequined sari. Hukum Chand felt a little foolish. The girl had been there two nights, and there she was sleeping all by herself in a chair. She was still, save for the gentle heaving of her bosom. He felt old and unclean. How could he have done anything to this child? If his daughter had lived, she would have been about the same age. He felt a pang of remorse. He also knew that his remorse and good resolutions went with the hangover. They always did. He would probably drink again and get the same girl over and sleep with her—and feel badly about it. That was life, and it was depressing.

He got up slowly and opened the attaché case that lay on the table. He looked at himself in the mirror on the inside of the lid. There was a yellow rheum in the corners of his eyes. The roots of his hair were showing white and purple. There were several folds of flesh under his unshaven jaw. He was old and ugly. He stuck out his tongue. It was coated with a smooth pale yellow from the middle to the back. Dribble ran down the tip onto the table. He could smell his own breath. It must have been nauseating for the girl! No wonder she spent the night in an uncomfortable chair. Hukum Chand took out a bottle of liver salts and put several large teaspoonfuls into a glass. He unscrewed the thermos flask and poured in the water. The effervescence bubbled over from all sides of the tumbler onto the table. He stirred the water till the fizz died down, then drank it quickly. For some time he stood with his head bent and his hands resting on the table.

The dose of salts gurgled down pleasantly. An airy fullness rose from the pit of his stomach up to his throat and burped out in a long satisfying belch. The throbbing ebbed away and the ache receded into the back of his head. A few cups of strong hot tea and he would be himself again. Hukum Chand went to the bathroom. From the door opening out toward the servants' quarters he shouted for his bearer.

"Bring shaving water and bring my tea. Bring it here. I will take it in myself."

When the bearer came, Hukum Chand took the tea tray and the mug of hot shaving water into the bedroom and put them on the table. He poured himself a cup of tea and laid out his shaving things. He lathered his chin and shaved and sipped his tea. The tinkle of the china and silver did not disturb the girl. She slept with her mouth slightly open. She looked dead except for the periodic upward movement of her breasts vainly trying to fill her bodice. Her hair was scattered all over her face. A pink celluloid clip made in the shape of a butterfly dangled by the leg of the chair. Her sari was crushed and creased, and bits of sequins glistened on the floor. Hukum Chand could not take his eyes off her while he sipped his tea and shaved. He could not analyze his feelings except that he wanted to make up to her. If she wanted to be slept with, he would sleep with her. The thought made him uneasy. He would have to drink hard to do that to her now.

The noise of shuffling feet and coughing on the verandah disturbed Hukum Chand's thoughts. It was a cough intended to draw attention. That meant the subinspector. Hukum Chand finished his tea and took his clothes into the bathroom to change. Afterward, he went out of the door which opened toward the quarters and stepped onto the verandah. The subinspector was reading a newspaper. He jumped up from his chair and saluted.

"Has your honor been out walking in the rain?"

"No, no. I just went round the servants' quarters. You are early. I hope all is well."

"These days one should be grateful for being alive. There is no peace anywhere. One trouble after another . . . "

The magistrate suddenly thought of the corpses. "Did it rain in the night? How is it going near the railway station?"

"I went by this morning when the rain had just started. There wasn't very much left—just a big heap of ashes and bones. There are many skulls lying about. I do not know what we can do about them. I have sent word to the lambardar that no one is to be allowed near the bridge or the railway station."

"How many were there? Did you count?"

"No, sir. The Sikh officer said there were more than a thousand. I think he just calculated how many people could get into a bogie and multiplied it by the number of bogies. He said that another four or five hundred must have been killed on the roofs, on footboards and between buffers. They must have fallen off when they were attacked. The roof was certainly covered with dried-up blood."

"Harey Ram, Harey Ram. Fifteen hundred innocent people! What else is Kalyug? There is darkness over the land. This is only one spot on the frontier. I suppose similar things are happening at other places. And now I believe our people are doing the same. What about the Muslims in these villages?"

"That is what I came to report, sir. Muslims of some villages have started leaving for the refugee camp. Chundunnugger has been partly evacuated. Pakistan army lorries with Baluchi and Pathan soldiers have been picking them up whenever information has been brought. But the Mano Majra Muslims are still there and this morning the lambardar reported the arrival of forty or fifty Sikh refugees who had crossed the river by the ford at dawn. They are putting up at the temple."

"Why were they allowed to stop?" asked Hukum Chand sharply. "You know very well the orders are that all incoming refugees must proceed to the camp at Jullundur. This is serious. They may start the killing in Mano Majra."

"No, sir, the situation is well in hand up till now. These refugees have not lost much in Pakistan and apparently no one molested them on the way. The Muslims of Mano Majra have been bringing them food at the temple. If others turn up who have been through massacres and have lost relations, then it will be a different matter. I had not thought of the river crossings. Usually, after the rains the river is a mile in breadth and there are no fords till November or December. We have hardly had any rain this year. There are several points where people can cross and I have not got enough policemen to patrol the riverside."

Hukum Chand looked across the rest-house grounds. The rain

was falling steadily. Little pools had begun to form in the ditches. The sky was a flat stretch of slate gray.

"Of course, if it keeps raining, the river will rise and there will not be many fords to cross. One will be able to control refugee movements over the bridges."

A crash of lightning and thunder emphasized the tempo of the rain. The wind blew a thin spray onto the verandah.

"But we must get the Muslims out of this area whether they like it or not. The sooner the better."

There was a long pause in the conversation. Both men sat staring into the rain. Hukum Chand began to speak again.

"One should bow before the storm till it passes. See the pampas grass! Its leaves bend before the breeze. The stem stands stiff in its plumed pride. When the storm comes it cracks and its white plume is scattered by the winds like fluffs of thistledown." After a pause he added, "A wise man swims with the current and still gets across."

The subinspector heard the platitudes with polite attention. He did not see their significance to his immediate problem. Hukum Chand noticed the blank expression on the police officer's face. He had to make things more plain.

"What have you done about Ram Lal's murder? Have you made any further arrests?"

"Yes, sir, Jugga budmash gave us the names yesterday. They are men who were at one time in his own gang: Malli and four others from village Kapura two miles down the river. But Jugga was not with them. I have sent some constables to arrest them this morning."

Hukum Chand did not seem to be interested. He had his eyes fixed somewhere far away.

"We were wrong about both Jugga and the other fellow." The subinspector went on: "I told you about Jugga's liaison with a Muslim weaver's girl. That kept him busy most nights. Malli threw bangles into Jugga's courtyard after the dacoity."

Hukum Chand still seemed far away.

"If your honor agrees, we might release Jugga and Iqbal after we have got Malli and his companions."

"Who are Malli and his companions, Sikh or Muslim?" asked Hukum Chand abruptly.

"All Sikhs."

The magistrate relapsed into his thoughts once more. After some time he began to talk to himself. "It would have been more convenient if they had been Mussulman. The knowledge of that and the agitator fellow being a Leaguer would have persuaded Mano Majra Sikhs to let their Muslims go."

There was another long pause. The plan slowly pieced itself together in the subinspector's mind. He got up without making any comment. Hukum Chand did not want to take any chances.

"Listen," he said. "Let Malli and his gang off without making any entry anywhere. But keep an eye on their movements. We will arrest them when we want to . . . And do not release the budmash or the other chap yet. We may need them."

The subinspector saluted.

"Wait. I haven't finished." Hukum Chand raised his hand. "After you have done the needful, send word to the commander of the Muslim refugee camp asking for trucks to evacuate Mano Majra Muslims."

The subinspector saluted once more. He was conscious of the honor Hukum Chand had conferred by trusting him with the execution of a delicate and complicated plan. He put on his raincoat.

"I should not let you go in this rain, but the matter is so vital that you should not lose any time," said Hukum Chand, still looking down at the ground.

"I know, sir." The subinspector saluted again. "I shall take action at once." He mounted his bicycle and rode away from the rest house onto the muddy road.

Hukum Chand sat on the verandah staring vacantly at the

rain falling in sheets. The right and wrong of his instructions did not weigh too heavily on him. He was a magistrate, not a missionary. It was the day-to-day problems to which he had to find answers. He had no need to equate them to some unknown absolute standard. There were not many "oughts" in his life. There were just the "is" 's. He took life as it was. He did not want to recast it or rebel against it. There were processes of history to which human beings contributed willy-nilly. He believed that an individual's conscious effort should be directed to immediate ends like saving life when endangered, preserving the social structure and honoring its conventions. His immediate problem was to save Muslim lives. He would do that in any way he could. Besides, so far he had not really done anything outrageous. Two men who had been arrested on the strength of warrants signed by him should have been arrested in any case. One was an agitator, the other a bad character. In troubled times, it would be necessary to detain them. If he could make a minor error into a major investment, it would really be a mistake to call it a mistake. Hukum Chand felt elated. If his plan could be carried out efficiently! If only he could himself direct the details, there would be no slips! His subordinates frequently did not understand his mind and landed him in complicated situations.

From inside the rest house came the sound of the bathroom door shutting and opening. Hukum Chand got up and shouted at the bearer to bring in breakfast.

The girl sat on the edge of the bed with her chin in her hands. She stood up and covered her head with the loose end of the sari. When Hukum Chand sat down in the chair, she sat down on the bed again with her eyes fixed on the floor. There was an awkward silence. After some time Hukum Chand mustered his courage, cleared his throat and said, "You must be hungry. I have sent for some tea."

The girl turned her large sad eyes on him. "I want to go home."

"Have something to eat and I will tell the driver to take you home. Where do you live?"

"Chundunnugger. Where the Inspector Sahib has his police station."

There was another long pause. Hukum Chand cleared his throat again. "What is your name?"

"Haseena. Haseena Begum."

"Haseena. You are *haseen*. Your mother has chosen your name well. Is that old woman your mother?"

The girl smiled for the first time. No one had paid her a compliment before. Now the Government itself had called her beautiful and was interested in her family.

"No, sir, she is my grandmother. My mother died soon after I was born."

"How old are you?"

"I don't know. Sixteen or seventeen. Maybe eighteen. I was not born literate. I could not record my date of birth."

She smiled at her own little joke. The magistrate smiled too. The bearer brought in a tray of tea, toast and eggs.

The girl got up to arrange the teacups and buttered a piece of toast. She put it on a saucer and placed it on the table in front of Hukum Chand.

"I will not eat anything. I have had my tea."

The girl pretended to be cross.

"If you do not eat, then I won't eat either," she said coquettishly. She put away the knife with which she was buttering the toast, and sat down on the bed.

The magistrate was pleased. "Now, do not get angry with me," he said. He walked up to her and put his arms round her shoulders. "You must eat. You had nothing last night."

The girl wriggled in his arms. "If you eat, I will eat. If you do not, I will not either."

"All right, if you insist." Hukum Chand helped the girl up with his arm around her waist and brought her to his side of the table. "We will both eat. Come and sit with me."

The girl got over her nervousness and sat in his lap. She put thickly buttered toast in his mouth and laughed when he said "Enough, enough" through his stuffed mouth. She wiped the butter off his mustache.

"How long have you been in this profession?"

"What a silly question to ask! Why, ever since I was born. My mother was a singer and her mother was a singer till as long back as we know."

"I do not mean singing. Other things," explained Hukum Chand, looking away.

"What do you mean, other things?" asked the girl haughtily. "We do not go about doing other things for money. I am a singer and I dance. I do not suppose you know what dancing and singing are. You just know about other things. A bottle of whisky and other things. That is all!"

Hukum Chand cleared his throat with a nervous cough. "Well . . . I did not do anything."

The girl laughed and pressed her hand on the magistrate's face. "Poor Magistrate Sahib. You had evil intentions, but you were tired. You snored like a railway engine." The girl drew her breath in noisily and imitated his snoring. She laughed more loudly.

Hukum Chand stroked the girl's hair. His daughter would have been sixteen, seventeen, or eighteen, if she had lived. But he had no feeling of guilt, only a vague sense of fulfillment. He did not want to sleep with the girl, or make love to her, or even to kiss her on the lips and feel her body. He simply wanted her to sleep in his lap with her head resting on his chest.

"There you go again with your deep thoughts," said the girl, scratching his head with her finger. She poured out a cup of tea and then poured it into the saucer. "Have some tea. It will stop you thinking." She thrust the saucerful of tea at him.

"No, no. I have had tea. You have it."

"All right. I will have tea and you have your thoughts."

The girl began to sip the tea noisily.

"Haseena." He liked repeating the name. "Haseena," he started again.

"Yes. But Haseena is only my name. Why don't you say something?"

Hukum Chand took the empty saucer from her hand and put it on the table. He drew the girl closer and pressed her head against his. He ran his fingers through her hair.

"You are Muslim?"

"Yes, I am Muslim. What else could Haseena Begum be? A bearded Sikh?"

"I thought Muslims from Chundunnugger had been evacuated. How have you managed to stay on?"

"Many have gone away, but the Inspector Sahib said we could stay till he told us to go. Singers are neither Hindu nor Muslim in that way. All communities come to hear me."

"Are there any other Muslims in Chundunnugger?"

"Well . . . yes," she faltered. "You can call them Muslim, Hindu or Sikh or anything, male or female. A party of *hijras* [hermaphrodites] are still there." She blushed.

Hukum Chand put his hand across her eyes.

"Poor Haseena is embarrassed. I promise I won't laugh. You are not Hindu or Muslim, but not in the same way as a hijra is not a Hindu or Muslim."

"Do not tease me."

"I won't tease you," he said removing his hand. She was still blushing. "Tell me why the hijras were spared."

"I will if you promise not to laugh at me."

"I promise."

The girl became animated.

"There was a child born to someone living in the Hindu locality. Without even thinking about communal troubles the hijras went there to sing. Hindus and Sikhs—I do not like Sikhs—got hold of them and wanted to kill them because they were Muslim." She stopped deliberately.

"What happened?" asked Hukum Chand eagerly.

The girl laughed and clapped her hands the way hijras do, stretching her fingers wide. "They started to beat their drums and sing in their raucous male voices. They whirled round so fast that their skirts flew in the air. Then they stopped and asked the leaders of the mob, 'Now you have seen us, tell us, are we Hindus or Muslims?' and the whole crowd started laughing—the whole crowd except the Sikhs."

Hukum Chand also laughed.

"That is not all. The Sikhs came with their kirpans and threatened them saying, 'We will let you go this time, but you must get out of Chundunnugger or we will kill you.' One of the hijras again clapped his hands and ran his finger in a Sikh's beard and asked, 'Why? Will all of you become like us and stop having children?' Even the Sikhs started laughing."

"That is a good one," said Hukum Chand. "But you should be careful while all this disturbance is going on. Stay at home for a few days."

"I am not frightened. We know so many people so well and then I have a big powerful Magistrate to protect me. As long as he is there no one can harm a single hair of my head."

Hukum Chand continued to run his hands through the girl's hair without saying anything. The girl looked up at him smiling mischievously. "You want me to go to Pakistan?"

Hukum Chand pressed her closer. A hot feverish feeling came over him. "Haseena." He cleared his throat again. "Haseena." Words would not come out of his mouth.

"Haseena, Haseena, Haseena. I am not deaf. Why don't you say something?"

"You will stay here today, won't you? You do not want to go away just yet?"

"Is that all you wanted to say? If you do not give me your car, I cannot go five miles in the rain. But if you make me sing or spend another night here you will have to give me a big bundle of notes."

Hukum Chand felt relieved.

"What is money?" he said with mock gallantry. "I am ready to lay down my life for you."

For a week, Iqbal was left alone in his cell. His only companions were the piles of newspapers and magazines. There was no light in his cell, nor was he provided with a lamp. He had to lie in the stifling heat listening to night noises—snores, occasional gunshots, and then more snoring. When it started to rain, the police station became more dismal than ever. There was nothing to see except rain falling incessantly, or sometimes a constable running across between the reporting rooms and the barracks. There was nothing to hear except the monotonous patter of raindrops, an occasional peal of thunder, and then more rain. He saw little of Jugga in the neighboring cell. On the first two evenings, some constables had taken Jugga out of his cell. They brought him back after an hour. Iqbal did not know what they had done to him. He didn't ask and Jugga said nothing. But his repartee with the policemen became more vulgar and more familiar than before.

One morning a party of five men were brought to the station in handcuffs. As soon as Jugga saw them he lost his temper and abused them. They protested and refused to leave the reporting room verandah. Iqbal wondered who the new prisoners were. From the snatches of conversation that he had overheard, it seemed that everyone was on a spree, killing and looting. Even in Chundunnugger, a few yards from the police station, there had been killing. Iqbal had seen the pink glow of fire and heard people yelling, but the police had made no arrests. The prisoners must be quite out of the ordinary. While he was trying to figure out who the newcomers were, his cell was unlocked and Jugga came in with a constable. Jugga was in a good humor.

"Sat Sri Akal, Babuji," he said. "I am going to be the servant of your feet. I will learn something."

"Iqbal Sahib," the constable added, relocking the cell, "teach this budmash how to go on the straight and narrow path."

"Get away with you," Jugga said. "Babuji thinks it is you and the Government who have made me a budmash. Isn't that so, Babuji?"

Iqbal did not answer. He put his feet in the extra chair and gazed at the pile of papers. Jugga took Iqbal's feet off the chair and began pressing them with his enormous hands.

"Babuji, my kismet has waked up at last. I will serve you if you teach me some English. Just a few sentences so that I can do a little 'git mit.'"

"Who is going to occupy the next cell?"

Jugga continued pressing Iqbal's feet and legs.

"I don't know," he answered hesitantly. "They tell me they have arrested Ram Lal's murderers."

"I thought they had arrested you for the murder," said Iqbal.

"Me, too," smiled Jugga, baring his row of even white teeth studded with gold points. "They always arrest me when anything goes wrong in Mano Majra. You see, I am a budmash."

"Didn't you kill Ram Lal?"

Jugga stopped pressing. He caught his ears with his hands and stuck out his tongue. "Toba, toba! Kill my own village banian? Babuji, who kills a hen which lays eggs? Besides, Ram Lal gave me money to pay lawyers when my father was in jail. I would not act like a bastard."

"I suppose they will let you off now."

"The police are the kings of the country. They will let me off when they feel like it. If they want to keep me in, they will trump up a case of keeping a spear without a license or going out of the village without permission—or just anything."

"But you were out of the village that night. Weren't you?"

Jugga sat down on his haunches, took Iqbal's feet in his lap, and started massaging his soles.

"I was out of the village," he answered with a mischievous

twinkle in his eye, "but I was not murdering anyone. I was being murdered."

Iqbal knew the expression. He did not want to encourage Jugga to make further disclosures. But once the subject had been suggested, there was no keeping Jugga back. He began to press Iqbal's feet with greater fervor.

"You have been in Europe many years?" asked Jugga lowering his voice.

"Yes, many," answered Iqbal, vainly trying to evade the inevitable.

"Then, Babuji," asked Jugga lowering his voice further, "you must have slept with many mem-sahibs. Yes?"

Iqbal felt irritated. It was not possible to keep Indians off the subject of sex for long. It obsessed their minds. It came out in their art, literature and religion. One saw it on the hoardings in the cities advertising aphrodisiacs and curatives for ill effects of masturbation. One saw it in the law courts and market places, where hawkers did a thriving trade selling oil made of the skin of sand lizards to put life into tired groins and increase the size of the phallus. One read it in the advertisements of quacks who claimed to possess remedies for barrenness and medicines to induce wombs to yield male children. One heard about it all the time. No people used incestuous abuse quite as casually as did the Indians. Terms like *sala*, wife's brother ("I would like to sleep with your sister"), and *susra*, father-in-law ("I would like to sleep with your daughter") were as often terms of affection for one's friends and relatives as expressions of anger to insult one's enemies. Conversation on any topic—politics, philosophy, sport—soon came down to sex, which everyone enjoyed with a lot of giggling and hand-slapping.

"Yes, I have." Iqbal said, casually. "With many."

"Wah, wah," exclaimed Jugga with enthusiasm and vigorous pressing of Iqbal's feet. "Wah, Babuji—great. You must have had lots of fun. The mem-sahibs are like houris from paradise—white and soft, like silk. All we have here are black buffaloes."

107

"There is no difference between women. As a matter of fact, white women are not very exciting. Are you married?"

"No, Babuji. Who will give his daughter to a budmash? I have to get my pleasure where I can get it."

"Do you get much of it?"

"Sometimes. . . . When I go to Ferozepur for a hearing and if I save money from lawyers and their clerks, I have a good time. I make a bargain for the whole night. Women think, as with other men, that means two, or at the most three times.'" He twirled his mustache. "But when Juggut Singh leaves them, they cry 'hai, hai,' touch their ears, say 'toba, toba,' and beg me in the name of God to leave them and take the money back."

Iqbal knew it was a lie. Most young men talked like that.

"When you get married, you will find your wife a match for you," Iqbal said. "You will be holding your ears and saying 'toba, toba.'"

"There is no fun in marriage, Babuji. Where is the time or place for fun? In summer, everyone sleeps out in the open and all you can do is to slip away for a little while and get over with things before your relations miss you. In winter, men and women sleep separately. You have to pretend to answer the call of nature at the same time at night."

"You seem to know a lot about it, without being married."

Jugga laughed. "I don't keep my eyes shut. Besides, even if I am not married, I do a married man's work."

"You also answer calls of nature by arrangement?"

Jugga laughed louder. "Yes, Babuji, I do. That is what has brought me to this lockup. But I say to myself: if I had not been out that night, I would not have had the good fortune of meeting you, Babuji. I would not have the chance to learn English from you. Teach me some 'git mit' like 'good morning.' Will you, Babuji-sahib?"

"What will you do with English?" Iqbal asked. "The sahibs have left. You should learn your own language."

Jugga did not seem pleased with the suggestion. For him,

education meant knowing English. Clerks and letter writers who wrote Urdu or Gurmukhi were literate, but not educated.

" I can learn that from anyone. Bhai Meet Singh has promised to teach me Gurmukhi, but I never seem to get started. Babuji, how many classes have you read up to? You must have passed the tenth?"

Tenth was the school-leaving examination.

"Yes, I have passed the tenth. Actually I have passed sixteen."

"Sixteen! Wah, wah! I have never met anyone who had done that. In our village only Ram Lal had done four. Now he is dead, the only one who can read anything is Meet Singh. In the neighboring villages they haven't even got a bhai. Our Inspector Sahib has only read up to seven and the Deputy Sahib to ten. Sixteen! You must have lots of brain."

Iqbal felt embarrassed at the effusive compliments.

"Can you read or write anything?" he asked.

"I? No. My uncle's son taught me a little verse he learned at school. It is half English and half Hindustani:

> Pigeon—*kabootur, oodan*—fly
> Look—*dekho, usman*—sky

Do you know this?"

"No. Didn't he teach you the alphabet?"

"The A. B. C.? He did not know it himself. He knew as much as I do:

> A. B. C. where have you been?
> Edward's dead, I went to mourn.

You must know this one?"

"No, I don't know this either."

"Well, you tell me something in English."

Iqbal obliged. He taught Jugga how to say "good morning" and "goodnight." When Jugga wanted to know the English for some of the vital functions of life, Iqbal became impatient. Then the five new prisoners were brought into the neighboring cell. Jugga's jovial mood vanished as fast as it had come.

By eleven o'clock the rain had dwindled to a drizzle. The day became brighter. The subinspector looked up from his driving. Some distance ahead of him, the clouds opened up, unfolding a rich blue sky. A shaft of sunlight slanted across the rain. Its saffron beams played about on the sodden fields. The rainbows spanned the sky, framing the town of Chundunnugger in a multicolored arc.

The subinspector drove faster. He wanted to get to the police station before his head constable made an entry about Malli's arrest. It would be awkward to have to tear off pages from the station diary and then face a whole lot of questions from some impertinent lawyer. The head constable was a man of experience, but after the arrests of Jugga and Iqbal the subinspector's confidence in him had been somewhat shaken. He could not be relied on to handle a situation which was not routine. Would he know where to lock up the prisoners? He was a peasant, full of awe of the educated middle class. He would not have the nerve to disturb Iqbal (in whose cell he had put a charpoy and a chair and table). And if he had put Jugga and Malli together in the other cell, they would by now have discussed the murder and dacoity and decided to help each other.

As the subinspector cycled into the police station, a couple of policemen sitting on a bench on the verandah got up to receive him. One took his cycle; the other helped him with his raincoat, murmuring something about having to go out in the rain.

"Duty," said the subinspector pompously, "duty. Rain is nothing. Even if there was an earthquake, duty first! Is the head constable back?"

"Yes, sir. He brought in Malli's gang a few minutes ago and has gone to his quarters to have tea."

"Has he made any entry in the daily diary?"

"No, sir, he said he would wait for you to do that."

The subinspector was relieved. He went into the reporting

room, hung his turban on a peg and sat down in a chair. The table was stacked with registers of all kinds. One large one with its yellow pages all divided into columns lay open before him. He glanced at the last entry. It was in his own hand, about his leaving Mano Majra rest house earlier that morning.

"Good," he said aloud, rubbing his hands. He slapped his thighs and ran both his hands across his forehead and through his hair. "Right," he said loudly to himself. "Right."

A constable brought him a cup of tea, stirring it all the time.

"Your clothes must be wet!" he said, putting the tea on the table and giving it a last violent stir.

The subinspector picked it up without looking at the constable. "Have you locked Malli's gang in the same cell as Jugga?"

"Toba! Toba!" exclaimed the constable, holding his hands up to his shoulder. "Sir, there would have been a murder in the police station. You should have been here when we brought Malli in. As soon as Jugga saw him he went mad. I have never heard such abuse. Mother, sister, daughter—he did not leave one out. He shook the bars till they rattled. We thought the door would come off its hinges. There was no question of putting Malli in there. And Malli would not have gone in, any more than a lamb would into a lion's cage."

The subinspector smiled. "Didn't Malli swear back?"

"No. He really looked frightened and kept saying that he had nothing to do with the Mano Majra dacoity. Jugga yelled back saying that he had seen him with his own eyes and he would settle scores with all of them and their mothers, sisters and daughters, once he was out. Malli said he was not afraid of him any more since all Jugga could do now was to sleep with his weaver girl. You should really have seen Jugga then! He behaved like an animal. His eyes turned red; he put his hand on his mouth and yelled; he beat his chest and shook the iron bars; he swore that he would tear Malli limb from limb. I have never seen anyone in a rage like that. We could not take any chances, so we kept Malli in the reporting room till Jugga's temper was down. Then we moved Jugga into the Babu's cell and put Malli's men in Jugga's."

"It must have been a good tamasha," said the subinspector with a grin. "We will have some more. I am going to release Malli's men."

The constable looked puzzled. Before he could ask any questions, the subinspector dismissed him with a lordly wave of the hand.

"Policy, you know! You will learn when you have been in the service as long as I have. Go and see if the head constable has had his tea. Say it is important."

A little later the head constable arrived, belching contentment. He had the smug expression of one ready to protest against any commendation of his efficiency. The subinspector ignored the modest smile the other wore and asked him to shut the door and sit down. The head constable's expression changed from contentment to concern. He shut the door and stood on the other side of the table. "Yes, sir. What are the orders?"

"Sit down. Sit down," the subinspector said. His voice was cool. "There is no hurry."

The head constable sat down.

The subinspector rotated the sharp end of a pencil in his ear and examined the brown wax which stuck to it. He got a cigarette out of his pocket and tapped its tip on the matchbox several times before lighting it. He sucked it noisily. The smoke poured out of his nostrils, rebounded off the table and spread into the room.

"Head Constable Sahib," he said at last, removing a tiny bit of tobacco from his tongue, "Head Constable Sahib, there are lots of things to be done today, and I want you to do them personally."

"Yes, sir," answered the head constable gravely.

"First, take Malli and his men to Mano Majra. Release them where the villagers can see them being released. Near the temple, perhaps. Then inquire casually from the villagers if anyone has seen Sultana or any of his gang about. You need not say why. Just make the inquiries."

"But, sir. Sultana and his lot went away to Pakistan. Everyone knows that."

The subinspector put the end of his pencil in his ear again and rubbed the wax on the table. He took a couple of pulls at the cigarette and this time pouted his lips and sent jets of smoke bounding off the register into the head constable's face.

"I do not know that Sultana has gone to Pakistan. Anyway, he left after the dacoity in Mano Majra. There is no harm in asking the villagers if they know when he left, is there?"

The head constable's face lit up.

"I understand, sir. Are there any other orders?"

"Yes. Also inquire from the villagers if they knew anything about the mischief the Muslim Leaguer Iqbal had been up to when he was in Mano Majra."

The head constable looked puzzled again.

"Sir, the Babu's name is Iqbal Singh. He is a Sikh. He has been living in England and had his long hair cut."

The subinspector fixed the head constable with a stare and smiled. "There are many Iqbals. I am talking of a Mohammed Iqbal, you are thinking of Iqbal Singh. Mohammed Iqbal can be a member of the Muslim League."

"I understand, sir," repeated the head constable, but he had not really understood. He hoped he would catch up with the scheme in due course. "Your orders will be carried out."

"Just one thing more," added the subinspector, getting up from the table. "Get a constable to take a letter from me to the commander of the Muslim refugee camp. Also, remind me to send some constables to Mano Majra tomorrow when the Pakistan army chaps come to evacuate Muslim villagers."

The head constable realized that this was meant to help him understand the plan. He made a mental note of it, saluted a second time and clicked his heels. "Yes, sir," he said, and went out.

The subinspector put on his turban. He stood by the door looking into the courtyard of the station. The railway creeper on the wall facing him had been washed by the rain. Its leaves glistened in the sun. Policemen's dormitories on the left side had rows of charpoys with bedding neatly rolled on them. Opposite the dormitories were the station's two cells—in reality just ordinary rooms with iron bars instead of bricks for the front wall. One could see everything inside them from anywhere in the courtyard. In the nearer cell, Iqbal sat in a chair with his feet on the charpoy, reading a magazine. Several newspapers lay scattered on the floor. Juggut Singh was sitting, holding the bars with his hands, idly staring at the policemen's quarters. In the other cell, Malli and his companions lay sprawled on the floor talking to each other. They got up as the head constable and three policemen with rifles entered carrying handcuffs. Juggut Singh took no notice of the policemen going into the adjoining cell. He thought that Malli was probably being taken to court for a hearing.

Malli had been shaken by Juggut Singh's outburst. He was frightened of Juggut Singh and would sooner have made peace on the other's terms than go about in fear of violence—for Jugga was the most violent man in the district. Juggut Singh's abuse had made that impossible. Malli was the leader of his own band and felt that, after Jugga's insults, he had to say something to regain his prestige in the eyes of his companions. He thought of several nasty things he could have said, if he had known that Juggut Singh was going to return his offer of friendship with abuse. He felt hurt and angry. If he got another chance he would give it back to Jugga, abuse for abuse. Iron bars separated them and in any case there were armed policemen about.

The policemen handcuffed Malli and his companions and linked all the handcuffs to one long chain attached to a constable's belt. The head constable led them away. Two men armed with rifles kept the rear. As they emerged from their cell, Jugga looked up at Malli and then looked away.

"You forget old friends," said Malli with mock friendliness. "You don't even look at us and we pine away for you."

His companions laughed. "Let him be. Let him be."

Jugga sat still with his eyes fixed on the ground.

"Why are you so angry, my dear? Why so sad? Is it somebody's love that torments your soul?"

"Come along, keep moving," said the policemen reluctantly. They were enjoying the scene.

"Why can't we say 'Sat Sri Akal' to our old friend? Sat Sri Akal, Sardar Juggut Singhji. Is there any message we can convey for you? A love message maybe? To the weaver's daughter?"

Jugga kept staring through the bars as if he had not heard. He turned pale with anger. All the blood drained from his face. His hands tightened around the iron bars.

Malli turned round to his smiling companions. "Sardar Juggut Singh seems a little upset today. He will not answer our 'Sat Sri Akal.' We do not mind. We will say 'Sat Sri Akal' to him again."

Malli joined his manacled hands and bent low near Juggut Singh's iron bar door and started loudly "Sat Sri . . ."

Jugga's hands shot through the bars and gripped Malli by the hair protruding from the back of his turban. Malli's turban fell off. Jugga yelled murderously and with a jerk brought Malli's head crashing against the bars. He shook Malli as a terrier shakes a piece of rag from side to side, forward and backward, smashing his head repeatedly against the bars. Each jerk was accompanied by abuse: "This to rape your mother. This your sister. This your daughter. This for your mother again. And this . . . and this."

Iqbal, who had been watching the earlier proceedings from his chair, stood up in a corner and started shouting to the policemen: "Why don't you do something? Don't you see he will kill the man?"

115

The policemen began to shout. One of them tried to push the butt end of his rifle in Jugga's face, but Jugga dodged. Malli's head was spattered with blood. His skull and forehead were bruised all over. He began to wail. The subinspector ran up to the cell and hit Jugga violently on the hand with his swagger stick several times. Jugga would not let go. The subinspector drew his revolver and pointed it at Jugga. "Let go, you swine, or I will shoot."

Jugga held up Malli's head with both his hands and spat in his face. He pushed him away with more abuse. Malli fell in a heap with his hair all over his face and shoulders. His companions helped him up and wiped the blood and spit off his face with his turban. He cried like a child, swearing all the time, "May your mother die . . . you son of a pig . . . I will settle this with you." Malli and his men were led away. Malli could be heard crying till he was a long way from the police station.

Jugga sank back into the stupor he had been in before he lost his temper. He examined the marks the subinspector's swagger stick had left on the back of his hands. Iqbal continued shouting agitatedly. Jugga turned round angrily. "Shut up, you babu! What have I done to you that you talk so much?"

Jugga had not spoken rudely to him before. That scared Iqbal all the more.

"Inspector Sahib, now that the other cell is vacant, can't you shift me there?" he pleaded.

The subinspector smiled contemptuously. "Certainly, Mr. Iqbal, we will do all we can to make you comfortable. Tables, chairs—an electric fan maybe?"

MANO MAJRA

WHEN it was discovered that the train had brought a full load of corpses, a heavy brooding silence descended on the village. People barricaded their doors and many stayed up all night talking in whispers. Everyone felt his neighbor's hand against him, and thought of finding friends and allies. They did not notice the clouds blot out the stars nor smell the cool damp breeze. When they woke up in the morning and saw it was raining, their first thoughts were about the train and the burning corpses. The whole village was on the roofs looking toward the station.

The train had disappeared as mysteriously as it had come. The station was deserted. The soldier's tents were soaked with water and looked depressing. There was no smoldering fire nor smoke. In fact there was no sign of life—or death. Still people watched; perhaps there would be another train with more corpses!

By afternoon the clouds had rolled away to the west. Rain had cleared the atmosphere and one could see for miles around. Villagers ventured forth from their homes to find out if anyone knew more than they. Then they went back to their roofs. Although it had stopped raining, no one could be seen on the station platform or in the passenger shed or the military camp. A row of vultures sat on the parapet of the station building and kites were flying in circles high above it.

The head constable, with his posse of policemen and prisoners, was spotted a long way away from the village. People shouted the information to each other. The lambardar was summoned.

117

When the head constable arrived with his party, there was quite a crowd assembled under the peepul tree near the temple.

The head constable unlocked the handcuffs of the prisoners in front of the villagers. They were made to put their thumb impressions on pieces of paper and told to report to the police station twice a week. The villagers looked on sullenly. They knew that Jugga budmash and the stranger had nothing to do with the dacoity. They were equally certain that in arresting Malli's gang the police were on the right track. Perhaps they were not all involved; some of the five might have been arrested mistakenly. It was scarcely possible that none of them had had anything to do with it. Yet there were the police letting them loose—not in their own village, but in Mano Majra where they had committed the murder. The police must be certain of their innocence to take such a risk.

The head constable took the lambardar aside and the two spoke to each other for some time. The lambardar came back and addressed the villagers saying: "The Sentry Sahib wants to know if anyone here has seen or heard anything about Sultana budmash or any of his gang."

Several villagers came out with news. He was known to have gone away to Pakistan along with his gang. They were all Muslims, and Muslims of their village had been evacuated.

"Was it before or after the murder of the Lala that he left?" inquired the head constable, coming up beside the lambardar.

"After," they answered in a chorus. There was a long pause. The villagers looked at each other somewhat puzzled. Was it them? Before they could ask the policemen any questions, the head constable was speaking again.

"Did any of you see or talk to a young Mussulman babu called Mohammed Iqbal who was a member of the Muslim League?"

The lambardar was taken aback. He did not know Iqbal was a Muslim. He vaguely recalled Meet Singh and Imam Baksh calling him Iqbal Singh. He looked in the crowd for Imam

Baksh but could not find him. Several villagers started telling the head constable excitedly of having seen Iqbal go to the fields and loiter about the railway track near the bridge.

"Did you notice anything suspicious about him?"

"Suspicious? Well . . . "

"Did you notice anything suspicious about the fellow?"

"Did you?"

No one was sure. One could never be sure about educated people; they were all suspiciously cunning. Surely Meet Singh was the one to answer questions about the babu; some of the babu's things were still with him in the gurdwara.

Meet Singh was pushed up to the front.

The head constable ignored Meet Singh and again addressed the group who had been answering him. "I will speak to the bhai later," he said. "Can any one of you say whether this man came to Mano Majra before or after the dacoity?"

This was another shock. What would an urban babu have to do with dacoity or murder? Maybe it was not for money after all! No one was quite sure. Now they were not sure of anything. The head constable dismissed the meeting with: "If anyone has any authentic information about the moneylender's murder or about Sultana or about Mohammed Iqbal, report at the police station at once."

The crowd broke into small groups, talking and gesticulating animatedly. Meet Singh went up to the head constable who was getting his constables ready to march back.

"Sentry Sahib, the young man you arrested the other day is not a Mussulman. He is a Sikh—Iqbal Singh."

The head constable took no notice of him. He was busy writing something on a piece of yellow paper. Meet Singh waited patiently.

"Sentry Sahib," he started again as the other was folding the paper. The head constable did not even look at him. He beckoned one of the constables and handed him the paper saying:

"Get a bicycle or a tonga and take this letter to the commandant of the Pakistan military unit. Also tell him yourself that you have come from Mano Majra and the situation is serious. He must send his trucks and soldiers to evacuate the Muslims as early as possible. At once."

"Yes, sir," answered the constable clicking his heels.

"Sentry Sahib," implored Meet Singh.

"Sentry Sahib, Sentry Sahib, Sentry Sahib," repeated the head constable angrily. "You have been eating my ears with your 'Sentry Sahibs.' What do you want?"

"Iqbal Singh is a Sikh."

"Did you open the fly-buttons of his pants to see whether he was a Sikh or a Mussulman? You are a simple bhai of a temple. Go and pray."

The head constable took his place in front of the policemen standing in double file.

"Attention! By the left, quick march."

Meet Singh turned back to the temple without answering the eager queries of the villagers.

The head constable's visit had divided Mano Majra into two halves as neatly as a knife cuts through a pat of butter.

Muslims sat and moped in their houses. Rumors of atrocities committed by Sikhs on Muslims in Patiala, Ambala and Kapurthala, which they had heard and dismissed, came back to their minds. They had heard of gentlewomen having their veils taken off, being stripped and marched down crowded streets to be raped in the market place. Many had eluded their would-be ravishers by killing themselves. They had heard of mosques being desecrated by the slaughter of pigs on the premises, and of copies of the holy Koran being torn up by infidels. Quite suddenly every Sikh in Mano Majra became a stranger with an evil intent. His long hair and beard appeared barbarous, his kirpan menacingly anti-Muslim. For the first time, the name Pakistan came to mean something to them—a haven of refuge where there were no Sikhs.

The Sikhs were sullen and angry. "Never trust a Mussulman," they said. The last Guru had warned them that Muslims had no loyalties. He was right. All through the Muslim period of Indian history, sons had imprisoned or killed their own fathers and brothers had blinded brothers to get the throne. And what had they done to the Sikhs? Executed two of their Gurus, assassinated another and butchered his infant children; hundreds of thousands had been put to the sword for no other offense than refusing to accept Islam; their temples had been desecrated by the slaughter of kine; the holy Granth had been torn to bits. And Muslims were never ones to respect women. Sikh refugees had told of women jumping into wells and burning themselves rather than fall into the hands of Muslims. Those who did not commit suicide were paraded naked in the streets, raped in public, and then murdered. Now a trainload of Sikhs massacred by Muslims had been cremated in Mano Majra. Hindus and Sikhs were fleeing from their homes in Pakistan and having to find shelter in Mano Majra. Then there was the murder of Ram Lal. No one knew who had killed him, but everyone knew Ram Lal was a Hindu; Sultana and his gang were Muslims and had fled to Pakistan. An unknown character—without turban or beard—had been loitering about the village. These were reasons enough to be angry with someone. So they decided to be angry with the Muslims; Muslims were basely ungrateful. Logic was never a strong point with Sikhs; when they were roused, logic did not matter at all.

It was a gloomy night. The breeze that had swept away the clouds blew them back again. At first they came in fleecy strands of white. The moon wiped them off its face. Then they came in large billows, blotted out the moonlight and turned the sky a dull gray. The moon fought its way through and occasionally patches of the plain sparkled like silver. Later, clouds came in monstrous black formations and spread across the sky. Then without any lightning or thunder it began to rain.

A group of Sikh peasants gathered together in the house of the lambardar. They sat in a circle around a hurricane lantern—some on a charpoy, others on the floor. Meet Singh was amongst them.

For a long time nobody said anything apart from repeating, "God is punishing us for our sins."

"Yes, God is punishing us for our sins."

"There is a lot of *zulum* in Pakistan."

"That is because He wants to punish us for our sins. Bad acts yield a bitter harvest."

Then one of the younger men spoke. "What have we done to deserve this? We have looked upon the Muslims as our brothers and sisters. Why should they send somebody to spy on us?"

"You mean Iqbal?" Meet Singh said. "I had quite a long conversation with him. He had an iron bangle on his wrist like all of us Sikhs and told me that his mother had wanted him to wear it, so he wore it. He is a shaven Sikh. He does not smoke. And he came the day after the moneylender's murder."

"Bhai, you get taken in easily," replied the same youth. "Does it hurt a Mussulman to wear an iron bangle or not smoke for a day—particularly if he has some important work to do?"

"I may be a simple bhai," protested Meet Singh warmly, "but I know as well as you that the babu had nothing to do with the murder; he would not have been in the village afterwards if he had. That any fathead would understand."

The youth felt a little abashed.

"Besides that," continued Meet Singh more confidently, "they had already arrested Malli for the dacoity . . . "

"How do you know what they had arrested Malli for?" interrupted the youth triumphantly.

"Yes, how do you know what the police know? They have released Malli. Have you ever known them to release murderers without a trial and acquittal?" asked some others.

"Bhai, you always talk without reason."

"Accha, if you are the ones with all the reason, tell me who threw the packet of bangles into Jugga's house."

"How should we know?" answered a chorus.

"I will tell you. It was Jugga's enemy Malli. You all know they had fallen out. Who else would dare insult Jugga except he?"

No one answered the question. Meet Singh went on aggressively to drive his point home. "And all this about Sultana, Sultana! What has that to do with the dacoity?"

"Yes, Bhaiji, you may be right," said another youth. "But Lala is dead: why bother about him? The police will do that. Let Jugga, Malli and Sultana settle their quarrels. As for the babu, for all we care he can sleep with his mother. Our problem is: what are we to do with all these pigs we have with us? They have been eating our salt for generations and see what they have done! We have treated them like our own brothers. They have behaved like snakes."

The temperature of the meeting went up suddenly. Meet Singh spoke angrily.

"What have they done to you? Have they ousted you from your lands or occupied your houses? Have they seduced your womenfolk? Tell me, what have they done?"

"Ask the refugees what they have done to them," answered the truculent youth who had started the argument. "You mean to tell us that they are lying when they say that gurdwaras have been burned and people massacred?"

"I was only talking of Mano Majra. What have our tenants done?"

"They are Muslims."

Meet Singh shrugged his shoulders.

The lambardar felt it was up to him to settle the argument.

"What had to happen has happened," he said wisely. "We have to decide what we are to do now. These refugees who have turned up at the temple may do something which will bring a bad name on the village."

The reference to "something" changed the mood of the meeting. How could outsiders dare do "something" to their fellow villagers? Here was another stumbling block to logic. Group loyalty was above reason. The youth who had referred to Muslims as pigs spoke haughtily: "We would like to see somebody raise his little finger against our tenants while we live!"

The lambardar snubbed him. "You are a hotheaded one. Sometimes you want to kill Muslims. Sometimes you want to kill refugees. We say something and you drag the talk to something else."

"All right, all right, Lambardara," retorted the young man, "if you are all that clever, you say something."

"Listen, brothers," said the lambardar lowering his voice. "This is no time to lose tempers. Nobody here wants to kill anyone. But who knows the intentions of other people? Today we have forty or fifty refugees, who by the grace of the Guru are a peaceful lot and they only talk. Tomorrow we may get others who may have lost their mothers or sisters. Are we going to tell them: 'do not come to this village'? And if they do come, will we let them wreak vengeance on our tenants?"

"You have said something worth a hundred thousand rupees," said an old man. "We should think about it."

The peasants thought about their problem. They could not refuse shelter to refugees: hospitality was not a pastime but a sacred duty when those who sought it were homeless. Could they ask their Muslims to go? Quite emphatically not! Loyalty to a fellow villager was above all other considerations. Despite the words they had used, no one had the nerve to suggest throwing them out, even in a purely Sikh gathering. The mood of the assembly changed from anger to bewilderment.

After some time the lambardar spoke.

"All Muslims of the neighboring villages have been evacuated and taken to the refugee camp near Chundunnugger. Some have already gone away to Pakistan. Others have been sent to the bigger camp at Jullundur."

"Yes," added another. "Kapoora and Gujjoo Matta were evacuated last week. Mano Majra is the only place left where there are Muslims. What I would like to know is how these people asked their fellow villagers to leave. We could never say anything like that to our tenants, any more than we could tell our sons to get out of our homes. Is there anyone here who could say to the Muslims, 'Brothers, you should go away from Mano Majra'?"

Before anyone could answer another villager came in and stood on the threshold. Everyone turned round to see, but they could not recognize him in the dim lamplight.

"Who is it?" asked the lambardar, shading his eyes from the lamp. "Come in."

Imam Baksh came in. Two others followed him. They also were Muslims.

"Salaam, Chacha Imam Baksh. Salaam Khair Dina. Salaam, salaam."

"Sat Sri Akal, Lambardara. Sat Sri Akal," answered the Muslims.

People made room for them and waited for Imam Baksh to begin.

Imam Baksh combed his beard with his fingers.

"Well, brothers, what is your decision about us?" he asked quietly.

There was an awkward silence. Everyone looked at the lambardar.

"Why ask us?" answered the lambardar. "This is your village as much as ours."

"You have heard what is being said! All the neighboring villages have been evacuated. Only we are left. If you want us to go too, we will go."

Meet Singh began to sniff. He felt it was not for him to speak. He had said his bit. Besides, he was only a priest who lived on what the villagers gave him. One of the younger men spoke.

"It is like this, Uncle Imam Baksh. As long as we are here

125

nobody will **dare to** touch you. We die first and then you can look after yourselves."

"Yes," added another warmly, "we first, then you. If anyone raises his eyebrows at you we will rape his mother."

"Mother, sister and daughter," added the others.

Imam Baksh wiped a tear from his eyes and blew his nose in the hem of his shirt.

"What have we to do with Pakistan? We were born here. So were our ancestors. We have lived amongst you as brothers." Imam Baksh broke down. Meet Singh clasped him in his arms and began to sob. Several of the people started crying quietly and blowing their noses.

The lambardar spoke: "Yes, you are our brothers. As far as we are concerned, you and your children and your grandchildren can live here as long as you like. If anyone speaks rudely to you, your wives or your children, it will be us first and our wives and children before a single hair of your heads is touched. But Chacha, we are so few and the strangers coming from Pakistan are coming in thousands. Who will be responsible for what they do?"

"Yes," agreed the others, "as far as we are concerned you are all right, but what about these refugees?"

"I have heard that some villages were surrounded by mobs many thousands strong, all armed with guns and spears. There was no question of resistance."

"We are not afraid of mobs," replied another quickly. "Let them come! We will give them such a beating they will not dare to look at Mano Majra again."

Nobody took notice of the challenger; the boast sounded too hollow to be taken seriously. Imam Baksh blew his nose again. "What do you advise us to do then, brothers?" he asked, choking with emotion.

"Uncle," said the lambardar in a heavy voice, "it is very hard for me to say, but seeing the sort of time we live in, I would advise you to go to the refugee camp while this trouble is on.

You lock your houses with your belongings. We will look after your cattle till you come back."

The lambardar's advice created a tense stillness. Villagers held their breath for fear of being heard. The lambardar himself felt that he ought to say something quickly to dispel the effect of his words.

"Until yesterday," he began again loudly, "in case of trouble we could have helped you to cross the river by the ford. Now it has been raining for two days; the river has risen. The only crossings are by trains and road bridges—you know what is happening there! It is for your own safety that I advise you to take shelter in the camp for a few days, and then you can come back. As far as we are concerned," he repeated warmly, "if you decide to stay on, you are most welcome to do so. We will defend you with our lives."

No one had any doubts about the import of the lambardar's words. They sat with their heads bowed till Imam Baksh stood up.

"All right," he said solemnly, "if we have to go, we better pack up our bedding and belongings. It will take us more than one night to clear out of homes it has taken our fathers and grandfathers hundreds of years to make."

The lambardar felt a strong sense of guilt and was overcome with emotion. He got up and embraced Imam Baksh and started to cry loudly. Sikh and Muslim villagers fell into each other's arms and wept like children. Imam Baksh gently got out of the lambardar's embrace. "There is no need to cry," he said between sobs. "This is the way of the world—

> *Not forever does the bulbul sing*
> *In balmy shades of bowers,*
> *Not forever lasts the spring*
> *Nor ever blossom flowers.*
> *Not forever reigneth joy,*

127

Sets the sun on days of bliss,
Friendships not forever last,
They know not life, who know not this.

"They know not life, who know not this," repeated many others with sighs. "Yes, Uncle Imam Baksh. This is life."

Imam Baksh and his companions left the meeting in tears.

Before going round to other Muslim homes, Imam Baksh went to his own hut attached to the mosque. Nooran was already in bed. An oil lamp burned in a niche in the wall.

"Nooro, Nooro," he shouted, shaking her by the shoulder. "Get up, Nooro."

The girl opened her eyes. "What is the matter?"

"Get up and pack. We have to go away tomorrow morning," he announced dramatically.

"Go away? Where?"

"I don't know . . . Pakistan!"

The girl sat up with a jerk. "I will not go to Pakistan," she said defiantly.

Imam Baksh pretended he had not heard. "Put all the clothes in the trunks and the cooking utensils in a gunny bag. Also take something for the buffalo. We will have to take her too."

"I will not go to Pakistan," the girl repeated fiercely.

"You may not want to go, but they will throw you out. All Muslims are leaving for the camp tomorrow."

"Who will throw us out? This is our village. Are the police and the government dead?"

"Don't be silly, girl. Do as you are told. Hundreds of thousands of people are going to Pakistan and as many coming out. Those who stay behind are killed. Hurry up and pack. I have to go and tell the others that they must get ready."

Imam Baksh left the girl sitting up in bed. Nooran rubbed her face with her hands and stared at the wall. She did not know

128

what to do. She could spend the night out and come back when all the others had gone. But she could not do it alone; and it was raining. Her only chance was Jugga. Malli had been released, maybe Jugga had also come home. She knew that was not true, but the hope persisted and it gave her something to do.

Nooran went out in the rain. She passed many people in the lanes, going about with gunny bags covering their heads and shoulders. The whole village was awake. In most houses she could see the dim flickers of oil lamps. Some were packing; others were helping them to pack. Most just talked with their friends. The women sat on the floors hugging each other and crying. It was as if in every home there had been a death.

Nooran shook the door of Jugga's house. The chain on the other side rattled but there was no response. In the gray light she noticed the door was bolted from the outside. She undid the iron ring and went in. Jugga's mother was out, probably visiting some Muslim friends. There was no light at all. Nooran sat down on a charpoy. She did not want to face Jugga's mother alone nor did she want to go back home. She hoped something would happen—something which would make Jugga walk in. She sat and waited and hoped.

For an hour Nooran watched the gray shadows of clouds chasing each other. It drizzled and poured and poured and drizzled alternately. She heard the sound of footsteps cautiously picking their way through the muddy lane. They stopped outside the door. Someone shook the door.

"Who is it?" asked an old woman's voice.

Nooran lost her nerve; she did not move.

"Who is it?" demanded the voice angrily. "Why don't you speak?"

Nooran stood up and mumbled indistinctly, "Beybey."

The old woman stepped in and quickly shut the door behind her.

"Jugga! Jugga, is it you?" she whispered. "Have they let you off?"

"No, Beybey, it is I—Nooran. Chacha Imam Baksh's daughter," answered the girl timidly.

"Nooro? What brings you here at this hour?" the old woman asked angrily.

"Has Jugga come back?"

"What have you to do with Jugga?" his mother snapped. "You have sent him to jail. You have made him a budmash. Does your father know you go about to strangers' houses at midnight like a tart?"

Nooran began to cry. "We are going away tomorrow."

That did not soften the old woman's heart.

"What relation are you to us that you want to come to see us? You can go where you like."

Nooran played her last card. "I cannot leave. Jugga has promised to marry me."

"Get out, you bitch!" the old woman hissed. "You, a Muslim weaver's daughter, marry a Sikh peasant! Get out, or I will go and tell your father and the whole village. Go to Pakistan! Leave my Jugga alone."

Nooran felt heavy and lifeless. "All right, Beybey, I will go. Don't be angry with me. When Jugga comes back just tell him I came to say 'Sat Sri Akal.'" The girl went down on her knees, clasped the old woman's legs and began to sob. "Beybey, I am going away and will never come back again. Don't be harsh to me just when I am leaving."

Jugga's mother stood stiff, without a trace of emotion on her face. Inside her, she felt a little weak and soft. "I will tell Jugga."

Nooran stopped crying. Her sobs came at long intervals. She still held onto Jugga's mother. Her head sank lower and lower till it touched the old woman's feet.

"Beybey."

"What have you to say now?" She had a premonition of what was coming.

"Beybey."

"Beybey! Beybey! Why don't you say something?" asked the woman, pushing Nooran away. "What is it?"

The girl swallowed the spittle in her mouth.

"Beybey, I have Jugga's child inside me. If I go to Pakistan they will kill it when they know it has a Sikh father."

The old woman let Nooran's head drop back on her feet. Nooran clutched them hard and began to cry again.

"How long have you had it?"

"I have just found out. It is the second month."

Jugga's mother helped Nooran up and the two sat down on the charpoy. Nooran stopped sobbing.

"I cannot keep you here," said the old woman at last. "I have enough trouble with the police already. When all this is over and Jugga comes back, he will go and get you from wherever you are. Does your father know?"

"No! If he finds out he will marry me off to someone or murder me." She started crying again.

"Oh, stop this whining," commanded the old woman sternly. "Why didn't you think of it when you were at the mischief? I have already told you Jugga will get you as soon as he is out."

Nooran stifled her sobs.

"Beybey, don't let him be too long."

"He will hurry for his own sake. If he does not get you he will have to buy a wife and there is not a pice or trinket left with us. He will get you if he wants a wife. Have no fear."

A vague hope filled Nooran's being. She felt as if she belonged to the house and the house to her; the charpoy she sat on, the buffalo, Jugga's mother, all were hers. She could come back even if Jugga failed to turn up. She could tell them she was married. The thought of her father came like a dark cloud over her lunar hopes. She would slip away without telling him. The moon shone again.

"Beybey, if I get the chance I will come to say 'Sat Sri Akal' in the morning. Sat Sri Akal. I must go and pack." Nooran hugged the old woman passionately. "Sat Sri Akal," she said a little breathlessly again and went out.

Jugga's mother sat on her charpoy staring into the dark for several hours.

Not many people slept in Mano Majra that night. They went from house to house—talking, crying, swearing love and friendship, assuring each other that this would soon be over. Life, they said, would be as it always had been.

Imam Baksh came back from his round of Muslim homes before Nooran had returned. Nothing had been packed. He was too depressed to be angry with her. It was as hard on the young as the old. She must have gone to see some of her friends. He started pottering around looking for gunny bags, tin canisters and trunks. A few minutes later Nooran came in.

"Have you seen all your girl friends? Let us get this done before we sleep," said Imam Baksh.

"You go to bed. I will put the things in. There is not much to do—and you must be tired," she answered.

"Yes, I am a little tired," he said sitting down on his charpoy. "You pack the clothes now. We can put in the cooking utensils in the morning after you have cooked something for the journey." Imam Baksh stretched himself on the bed and fell asleep.

There was not much for Nooran to do. A Punjabi peasant's baggage consists of little besides a change of clothes, a quilt and a pillow, a couple of pitchers, cooking utensils, and perhaps a brass plate and a copper tumbler or two. All that can be put on the only piece of furniture they possess—a charpoy. Nooran put her own and her father's clothes in a gray battered steel trunk which had been with them ever since she could remember. She lit a fire in the hearth to bake a few chapatties for the next day. Within half an hour she had done the cooking. She rinsed the utensils and put them in a gunny bag. Flour, salt and the spices that remained went in biscuit and cigarette tins, which in their turn went inside an empty kerosene oil can with a wood top. The packing was over. All that remained was to roll her quilt round the pillow, put the odds and ends on the charpoy and the charpoy on the buffalo. She could carry the piece of broken mirror in her hand.

It rained intermittently all night. Early in the morning it became a regular downpour. Villagers who had stayed up most of the night fell asleep in the monotonous patter of rain and the opiate of the fresh morning breeze.

The tooting of motor horns and the high note of truck engines in low gear plowing their way through the slush and mud woke the entire village. The convoy went around Mano Majra looking for a lane wide enough to let their trucks in. In front was a jeep fitted with a loud-speaker. There were two officers in it—a Sikh (the one who had come after the ghost train) and a Muslim. Behind the jeep were a dozen trucks. One of the trucks was full of Pathan soldiers and another one full of Sikhs. They were all armed with sten guns.

The convoy came to a halt outside the village. Only the jeep could make its way through. It drove up to the center and stopped beside the platform under the peepul tree. The two officers stepped out. The Sikh asked one of the villagers to fetch the lambardar. The Muslim was joined by the Pathan soldiers. He sent them out in batches of three to knock at every door and ask the Muslims to come out. For a few minutes Mano Majra echoed to cries of "All Muslims going to Pakistan come out at once. Come! All Muslims. Out at once."

Slowly the Muslims began to come out of their homes, driving their cattle and their bullock carts loaded with charpoys, rolls of bedding, tin trunks, kerosene oil tins, earthen pitchers and brass utensils. The rest of Mano Majra came out to see them off.

The two officers and the lambardar were the last to come out

133

of the village. The jeep followed them. They were talking and gesticulating animatedly. Most of the talking was between the Muslim officer and the lambardar.

"I have no arrangement to take all this luggage with bullock carts, beds, pots and pans. This convoy is not going to Pakistan by road. We are taking them to the Chundunnugger refugee camp and from there by train to Lahore. They can only take their clothes, bedding, cash and jewelry. Tell them to leave everything else here. You can look after it."

The news that the Mano Majra Muslims were going to Pakistan came as a surprise. The lambardar had believed they would only go to the refugee camp for a few days and then return.

"No, Sahib, we cannot say anything," replied the lambardar. "If it was for a day or two we could look after their belongings. As you are going to Pakistan, it may be many months before they return. Property is a bad thing; it poisons people's minds. No, we will not touch anything. We will only look after their houses."

The Muslim officer was irritated. "I have no time to argue. You see yourself that all I have is a dozen trucks. I cannot put buffaloes and bullock carts in them."

"No, Sahib," retorted the lambardar stubbornly. "You can say what you like and you can be angry with us, but we will not touch our brothers' properties. You want us to become enemies?"

"Wah, wah, Lambardar Sahib," answered the Muslim laughing loudly. "Shabash! Yesterday you wanted to kill them, today you call them brothers. You may change your mind again tomorrow."

"Do not taunt us like this, Captain Sahib. We are brothers and will always remain brothers."

"All right, all right, Lambardara. You are brothers," the officer said. "I grant you that, but I still cannot take all this stuff. You consult the Sardar Officer and your fellow villagers about it. I will deal with the Muslims."

The Muslim officer got on the jeep and addressed the crowd. He chose his words carefully.

"We have a dozen trucks and all you people who are going to Pakistan must get on them in ten minutes. We have other villages to evacuate later on. The only luggage you can take with you is what you can carry—nothing more. You can leave your cattle, bullock carts, charpoys, pitchers, and so on with your friends in the village. If we get a chance, we will bring these things out for you later. I give you ten minutes to settle your affairs. Then the convoy will move."

The Muslims left their bullock carts and thronged round the jeep, protesting and talking loudly. The Muslim officer who had stepped off the jeep went back to the microphone.

"Silence! I warn you, the convoy will move in ten minutes; whether you are on it or not will be no concern of mine."

Sikh peasants who had stood apart heard the order and went up to the Sikh officer for advice. The officer took no notice of them; he continued staring contemptuously over the upturned collar of his raincoat at the men, cattle, carts and trucks steaming in the slush and rain.

"Why, Sardar Sahib," asked Meet Singh nervously, "is not the lambardar right? One should not touch another's property. There is always danger of misunderstanding."

The officer looked Meet Singh up and down.

"You are quite right, Bhaiji, there is some danger of being misunderstood. One should never touch another's property; one should never look at another's woman. One should just let others take one's goods and sleep with one's sisters. The only way people like you will understand anything is by being sent over to Pakistan: have your sisters and mothers raped in front of you, have your clothes taken off, and be sent back with a kick and spit on your behinds."

The officer's speech was a slap in the face to all the peasants. But someone sniggered. Everyone turned around to look. It was Malli with his five companions. With them were a few young refugees who were staying at the Sikh temple. None of them belonged to Mano Majra.

"Sir, the people of this village are famous for their charity," said Malli smiling. "They cannot look after themselves, how can they look after other people? But do not bother, Sardar Sahib, we will take care of Muslim property. You can tell the other officer to leave it with us. It will be quite safe if you can detail some of your soldiers to prevent looting by these people."

There was complete confusion. People ran hither and thither shouting at the tops of their voices. Despite the Muslim officer's tone of finality, villagers clamored around him protesting and full of suggestions. He came up to his Sikh colleague surrounded by his bewildered coreligionists.

"Can you make arrangements for taking over what is left behind?"

Before the Sikh could answer, a babel of protests burst from all sides. The Sikh remained tight-lipped and aloof.

The Muslim officer turned around sharply. "Shut up!" he yelled.

The murmuring died down. He spoke again, punctuating each word with a stab of his forefinger.

"I give you five minutes to get into the trucks with just as much luggage as you can carry in your hands. Those who are not in will be left behind. And this is the last time I will say it."

"It is all settled," said the Sikh officer, speaking softly in Punjabi. "I have arranged that these people from the next village will look after the cattle, carts, and houses till it is over. I will have a list made and sent over to you."

His colleague did not reply. He had a sardonic smile on his face. Mano Majra Sikhs and Muslims looked on helplessly.

There was no time to make arrangements. There was no time even to say good-by. Truck engines were started. Pathan soldiers rounded up the Muslims, drove them back to the carts for a brief minute or two, and then onto the trucks. In the confusion of rain, mud and soldiers herding the peasants about with the muzzles of their sten guns sticking in their backs, the villagers saw little of each other. All they could do was to shout their last farewells from the trucks. The Muslim officer drove his jeep round the convoy to see that all was in order and then came to say good-by to his Sikh colleague. The two shook hands mechanically, without a smile or a trace of emotion. The jeep took its place in front of the line of trucks. The microphone blared forth once more to announce that they were ready to move. The officer shouted "Pakistan!" His soldiers answered in a chorus "Forever!" The convoy slushed its way toward Chundunnugger. The Sikhs watched them till they were out of sight. They wiped the tears off their faces and turned back to their homes with heavy hearts.

Mano Majra's cup of sorrow was not yet full. The Sikh officer summoned the lambardar. All the villagers came with him—no one wanted to be left alone. Sikh soldiers threw a cordon round them. The officer told the villagers that he had decided to appoint Malli custodian of the evacuated Muslims' property. Anyone interfering with him or his men would be shot.

Malli's gang and the refugees then unyoked the bullocks, looted the carts, and drove the cows and buffaloes away.

KARMA

ALL that morning, people sat in their homes and stared despondently through their open doors. They saw Malli's men and the refugees ransack Muslim houses. They saw Sikh soldiers come and go as if on their beats. They heard the piteous lowing of cattle as they were beaten and dragged along. They heard the loud cackle of hens and roosters silenced by the slash of the knife. But they did nothing but sit and sigh.

A shepherd boy, who had been out gathering mushrooms, came back with the news that the river had risen. No one took any notice of him. They only wished that it would rise more and drown the whole of Mano Majra along with them, their women, children, and cattle—provided it also drowned Malli, his gang, the refugees, and the soldiers.

While the men sighed and groaned, the rain fell in a steady downpour and the Sutlej continued to rise. It spread on either side of the central piers which normally contained the winter channel, and joined the pools round the other piers into one broad stream. It stretched right across the bridge, licking the dam which separated it from the fields of Mano Majra. It ran over the many little islands in the river bed till only the tops of the bushes that grew on them could be seen. Colonies of cormorants and terns which were used to roosting there flew over to the banks and then to the bridge—over which no trains had run for several days.

In the afternoon, another villager went around to the houses shouting "Oi Banta Singh, the river is rising! Oi Daleep Singha, the river has risen! Oi listen, it is already up to the dam!" The people just looked up with their melancholy eyes signifying, "We have heard that before." Then another man came with the same message, "The river has risen"; then another, and another, till everyone was saying "Do you know, the river has risen!"

At last the lambardar went out to see for himself. Yes, the river had risen. Two days of rain could not have caused it; it must have poured in the mountains after the melting of the snows. Sluice gates of canals had probably been closed to prevent the flood from bursting their banks; so there was no outlet except the river. The friendly sluggish stream of gray had become a menacing and tumultuous spread of muddy brown. The piers of the bridge were all that remained solid and contemptuously defiant of the river. Their pointed edges clove through the sheet of water and let it vent its impotent rage in a swirl of eddies and whirlpools. Rain beat upon the surface, pockmarking it all over. The Sutlej was a terrifying sight.

By evening, Mano Majra had forgotten about its Muslims and Malli's misdeeds. The river had become the main topic of conversation. Once more women stood on the rooftops looking to the west. Men started going in turns to the embankment to report on the situation.

Before sunset the lambardar went up again to see the river. It had risen more since his visit in the afternoon. Some of the clusters of pampas which had been above the water level were now partly submerged. Their stalks had gone limp and their sodden snow-white plumes floated on the water. He had never known the Sutlej to rise so high in so short a time. Mano Majra was still a long way off and the mud dam looked solid and safe. Nevertheless he arranged for watch to be kept all through the night. Four parties of three men each were to take turns and be on the embankment from sunset to sunrise and report every hour. The rest were to stay in their houses.

The lambardar's decision was a quilt under which the village slept snug and safe. The lambardar himself had little sleep. Soon after midnight the three men on watch came back talking loudly, in a high state of excitement. They could not tell in the gray muffled moonlight whether the river had risen more, but they had heard human voices calling for help. The cries came from over the water. They may have been from the other side or from the river itself. The lambardar went out with them. He took his chromium-plated flashlight.

The four men stood on the embankment and surveyed the Sutlej, which looked like a sheet of black. The white beam of the lambardar's torch scanned the surface of the river. They could see nothing but the swirling water. They held their breath and listened, but they could hear nothing except the noise of the rain falling on the water. Each time the lambardar asked if they were sure that what they had heard were human voices and not jackals, they felt more and more uncertain and had to ask each other: "It was clear, wasn't it, Karnaila?"

"Oh yes. It was clear enough. 'Hai, hai'—like someone in pain."

The four men sat under a tree, huddled around a hurricane lamp. The gunny sacks they used as raincoats were soaking wet; so were all their clothes. An hour later there was a break in the clouds. The rain slowed down to a drizzle and then stopped. The moon broke through the clouds just above the western horizon. Its reflection on the river made a broad path of shimmering tinfoil running from the opposite bank to the men under the tree. On this shining patch of moonlight even little ripples of water could be seen distinctly.

A black oval object hit the bridge pier and was swept by the stream towards the Mano Majra embankment. It looked like a big drum with sticks on its sides. It moved forward, backward and sideways until the current caught it again and brought it into the silvery path not far from where the men were sitting. It was a dead cow with its belly bloated like a massive barrel and its legs stiffly stretched upward. Then followed some blocks of thatch straw and bundles of clothing.

"It looks as if some village had been swept away by the flood," said the lambardar.

"Quiet! Listen!" said one of the villagers in a whisper. The faint sound of a moan was wafted across the waters.

"Did you hear?"

"Quiet!"

They held their breath and listened.

No, it could not have been human. There was a rumbling sound. They listened again. Of course, it was a rumble; it was a train. Its puffing became clearer and clearer. Then they saw the outlines of the engine and the train itself. It had no lights. There was not even a headlight on the engine. Sparks flew out of the engine funnel like fireworks. As the train came over the bridge, cormorants flew silently down the river and terns flew up with shrill cries. The train came to a halt at Mano Majra station. It was from Pakistan.

"There are no lights on the train."

"The engine did not whistle."

"It is like a ghost."

"In the name of the Lord do not talk like this," said the lambardar. "It may be a goods train. It must have been the siren you heard. These new American engines wail like someone being murdered."

"No, Lambardar, we heard the sound more than an hour ago; and again the same one before the train came on," replied one of the villagers.

"You cannot hear it any more. The train is not making any noise now."

From across the railway line, where some days earlier over a thousand dead bodies had been burned, a jackal sent up a long plaintive howl. A pack joined him. The men shuddered.

"Must have been the jackals. They sound like women crying when somebody dies," said the lambardar.

"No, no," protested the other. "No, it was a human voice as clear as you are talking to me now."

They sat and listened and watched strange undistinguishable forms floating on the floodwaters. The moon went down. After a brief period of darkness the eastern horizon turned gray. Long lines of bats flew across noiselessly. Crows began to caw in their sleep. The shrill cry of a koel came bursting through a clump of trees and all the world was awake.

The clouds had rolled away to the north. Slowly the sun came up and flooded the rain-soaked plain with a dazzling orange brilliance; everything glistened in the sunlight. The river had risen further. Its turbid water carried carts with the bloated carcasses of bulls still yoked to them. Horses rolled from side to side as if they were scratching their backs. There were also men and women with their clothes clinging to their bodies; little children sleeping on their bellies with their arms clutching the water and their tiny buttocks dipping in and out. The sky was soon full of kites and vultures. They flew down and landed on the floating carcasses. They pecked till the corpses themselves rolled over and shooed them off with hands which rose stiffly into the air and splashed back into the water.

"Some villages must have been flooded at night," said the lambardar gravely.

"Who yokes bulls to carts at night?" asked one of his companions.

"Yes, that is true. Why should the bullocks be yoked?"

More human forms could be seen coming through the arches of the bridge. They rebounded off the piers, paused, pirouetted at the whirlpools, and then came bouncing down the river. The men moved up toward the bridge to see some corpses which had drifted near the bank.

They stood and stared.

"Lambardara, they were not drowned. They were murdered."

An old peasant with a gray beard lay flat on the water. His arms were stretched out as if he had been crucified. His mouth was wide open and showed his toothless gums, his eyes were covered with film, his hair floated about his head like a halo. He had a deep wound on his neck which slanted down from the side to the chest. A child's head butted into the old man's armpit. There was a hole in its back. There were many others coming down the river like logs hewn on the mountains and cast into streams to be carried down to the plains. A few passed through the middle of the arches and sped onward faster. Others bumped into the piers and turned over to show their wounds till the current turned them over again. Some were without limbs, some had their bellies torn open, many women's breasts were slashed. They floated down the sunlit river, bobbing up and down. Overhead hung the kites and vultures.

The lambardar and the villagers drew the ends of their turbans across their faces. "The Guru have mercy on us," someone whispered. "There has been a massacre somewhere. We must inform the police."

"Police?" a small man said bitterly. "What will they do? Write a first information report?"

Sick and with heavy hearts, the party turned back to Mano Majra. They did not know what to say to people when they got back. The river had risen further? Some villages had been flooded? There had been a massacre somewhere upstream? There were hundreds of corpses floating on the Sutlej? Or, just keep quiet?

When they came back to the village nobody was about to hear what they had to say. They were all on the rooftops looking at the station. After several days a train had drawn up at Mano Majra in the daytime. Since the engine faced eastward, it must have come from Pakistan. This time too the place was full of soldiers and policemen and the station had been cordoned off. The news of the corpses on the river was shouted from the housetops. People told each other about the mutilation of women and children. Nobody wanted to know who the dead people were nor wanted to go to the river to find out. There was a new interest at the station, with promise of worse horrors than the last one.

There was no doubt in anyone's mind what the train contained. They were sure that the soldiers would come for oil and wood. They had no more oil to spare and the wood they had left was too damp to burn. But the soldiers did not come. Instead, a bulldozer arrived from somewhere. It began dragging its lower jaw into the ground just outside the station on the Mano Majra side. It went along, eating up the earth, chewing it, casting it aside. It did this for several hours, until there was a rectangular trench almost fifty yards long with mounds of earth on either side. Then it paused for a break. The soldiers and policemen who had been idly watching the bulldozer at work were called to order and marched back to the platform. They came back in twos carrying canvas stretchers. They tipped the stretchers into the pit and went back to the train for more. This went on all day till sunset. Then the bulldozer woke up again. It opened its jaws and ate up the earth it had thrown out before and vomited it into the trench till it was level with the ground. The place looked like the scar of a healed-up wound. Two soldiers were left to guard the grave from the depredations of jackals and badgers.

That evening, the entire village turned up for the evening prayers at the gurdwara. This had never happened before, except on Gurus' birthdays or on the New Year's Day in April. The only regular visitors to the temple were old men and women. Others came to have their children named, for baptisms, weddings and funerals. Attendance at prayers had been steadily going up since the murder of the moneylender; people did not want to be alone. Since the Muslims had gone, their deserted houses with doors swinging wide open had acquired an eerie, haunted look. Villagers walked past them quickly without turning their heads. The one place of refuge to which people could go without much explanation was the gurdwara. Men came pretending that they would be needed; women just to be with them, and they brought the children. The main hall where the scripture was kept and the two rooms on the side were jammed with refugees and villagers. Their shoes were neatly arranged in rows on the other side of the threshold.

Meet Singh read the evening prayer by the light of the hurricane lamp. One of the men stood behind him waving a fly whisk. When the prayer was over, the congregation sang a hymn while Meet Singh folded the Granth in gaudy silk scarfs and laid it to rest for the night. The worshipers stood up and folded their hands. Meet Singh took his place in front. He repeated the names of the ten Gurus, the Sikh martyrs and the Sikh shrines, and invoked their blessing; the crowd shouted their amens with loud "Wah Guru"'s at the end of each supplication. They went down on their knees, rubbed their foreheads on the ground, and the ceremony was over. Meet Singh came and joined the men.

It was a solemn assembly. Only the children played. They chased each other around the room, laughing and arguing. The adults scolded the children. One by one, the children returned to their mothers' laps and fell asleep. Then the men and women also stretched themselves on the floor in different parts of the room.

The day's events were not likely to be forgotten in sleep. Many could not sleep at all. Others slept fitfully and woke up with startled cries if a neighbor's leg or arm so much as touched them. Even the ones who snored with apparent abandon, dreamed and relived the scenes of the day. They heard the sound of motor vehicles, the lowing of cattle and people crying. They sobbed in their sleep and their beards were moist with their tears.

When the sound of a motor horn was heard once more, those who were awake but drowsy thought they were dreaming. Those that were dreaming thought they were hearing it in their dreams. In their dreams they even said "Yes, yes" to the voice which kept asking "Are you all dead?"

The late night visitor was a jeep like the one in which the army officers had come in the morning. It seemed to know its way about the village. It went from door to door with a voice inquiring "Is there anyone there?" Only the dogs barked in reply. Then it came to the temple and the engine was switched off. Two men walked into the courtyard and shouted again: "Is there anyone here or are you all dead?"

Everyone got up. Some children began to cry. Meet Singh turned up the wick of his hurricane lantern. He and the lambardar went out to meet the visitors.

The men saw the commotion they had created. They ignored the lambardar and Meet Singh and walked up to the threshold of the large room. One looked in at the bewildered crowd and asked:

"Are you all dead?"

"Any one of you alive?" added the other.

The lambardar answered angrily, "No one is dead in this village. What do you want?"

Before the men could answer two of their companions joined them. All were Sikhs. They wore khaki uniforms and had rifles slung on their shoulders.

"This village looks quite dead," repeated one of the strangers, loudly addressing his own companions.

"The Guru has been merciful to this village. No one has died here," answered Meet Singh with quiet dignity.

"Well, if the village is not dead, then it should be. It should be drowned in a palmful of water. It consists of eunuchs," said the visitor fiercely with a flourish of his hand.

The strangers took off their shoes and came inside the large hall. The lambardar and Meet Singh followed them. Men sat up and tied their turbans. Women put their children in their laps and tried to rock them to sleep again.

One of the group, who appeared to be the leader, motioned the others to sit down. Everyone sat down. The leader had an aggressive bossy manner. He was a boy in his teens with a little beard which was glued to his chin with brilliantine. He was small in size, slight of build and altogether somewhat effeminate;

a glossy red ribbon showed under the acute angle of his bright blue turban. His khaki army shirt hung loosely from his round drooping shoulders. He wore a black leather Sam Browne: the strap across his narrow chest charged with bullets and the broad belt clamped about his still narrower waist. On one side it had a holster with the butt of a revolver protruding; on the other side there was a dagger. He looked as if his mother had dressed him up as an American cowboy.

The boy caressed the holster of his revolver and ran his fingers over the silver noses of the bullets. He looked around him with complete confidence.

"Is this a Sikh village?" he asked insolently. It was obvious to the villagers that he was an educated city-dweller. Such men always assumed a superior air when talking to peasants. They had no regard for age or status.

"Yes, sir," answered the lambardar. "It has always been a Sikh village. We had Muslim tenants but they have gone."

"What sort of Sikhs are you?" asked the boy, glowering menacingly. He elaborated his question: "Potent or impotent?"

No one knew what to say. No one protested that this was not the sort of language one used in a gurdwara with women and children sitting by.

"Do you know how many trainloads of dead Sikhs and Hindus have come over? Do you know of the massacres in Rawalpindi and Multan, Gujranwala and Sheikhupura? What are you doing about it? You just eat and sleep and you call yourselves Sikhs— the brave Sikhs! The martial class!" he added, raising both his arms to emphasize his sarcasm. He surveyed his audience with his bright eyes daring anyone to contradict him. People looked down somewhat ashamed of themselves.

"What can we do, Sardarji?" questioned the lambardar. "If our government goes to war against Pakistan, we will fight. What can we do sitting in Mano Majra?"

"Government!" sneered the boy contemptuously. "You expect the government to do anything? A government consisting of cowardly banian moneylenders! Do the Mussulmans in Pakistan apply for permission from their government when they rape your sisters? Do they apply for permission when they stop trains and kill everyone, old, young, women and children? You want the government to do something! That is great! Shabash! Bravo!" He gave the holster on his side a jaunty smack.

"But, Sardar Sahib," said the lambardar falteringly, "Do tell us what we can do."

"That is better," answered the lad. "Now we can talk. Listen and listen very carefully." He paused, looked around and started again. He spoke slowly, emphasizing each sentence by stabbing the air with his forefinger. "For each Hindu or Sikh they kill, kill two Mussulmans. For each woman they abduct or rape, abduct two. For each home they loot, loot two. For each trainload of dead they send over, send two across. For each road convoy that is attacked, attack two. That will stop the killing on the other side. It will teach them that we also play this game of killing and looting."

He stopped to gauge the effect he had created. People listened to him with rapt openmouthed attention. Only Meet Singh did not look up; he cleared his throat but stopped.

"Well, brother, why do you keep quiet?" asked the lad, throwing a challenge.

"I was going to say," said Meet Singh haltingly, "I was going to say," he repeated, "what have the Muslims here done to us for us to kill them in revenge for what Muslims in Pakistan are doing? Only people who have committed crimes should be punished."

The lad glared angrily at Meet Singh. "What had the Sikhs and Hindus in Pakistan done that they were butchered? Weren't they innocent? Had the women committed crimes for which they were ravished? Had the children committed murder for which they were spiked in front of their parents?"

Meet Singh was subdued. The boy wanted to squash him further. "Why, brother? Now speak and say what you want to."

149

"I am an old Bhai; I could not lift my hands against anyone
—fight in battle or kill the killer. What bravery is there in
killing unarmed innocent people? As for women, you know that
the last Guru, Gobind Singh, made it a part of a baptismal oath
that no Sikh was to touch the person of a Muslim woman. And
God alone knows how he suffered at the hands of the Mussulmans! They killed all his four sons."

"Teach this sort of Sikhism to someone else," snapped the
boy contemptuously. "It is your sort of people who have been
the curse of this country. You quote the Guru about women;
why don't you tell us what he said about the Mussulmans? 'Only.
befriend the Turk when all other communities are dead.' Is that
correct?"

"Yes," answered Meet Singh meekly, "but nobody is asking
you to befriend them. Besides, the Guru himself had Muslims
in his army . . . "

"And one of them stabbed him while he slept."

Meet Singh felt uneasy.

"One of them stabbed him while he slept," repeated the boy.

"Yes . . . but there are bad ones and . . . "

"Show me a good one."

Meet Singh could not keep up with repartee. He just looked
down at his feet. His silence was taken as an admission of
defeat.

"Let him be. He is an old bhai. Let him stick to his prayers,"
said many in a chorus.

The speaker was appeased. He addressed the assembly again
in pompous tones. "Remember," he said like an oracle, "remember and never forget—a Muslim knows no argument but the
sword."

The crowd murmured approval.

"Is there anyone beloved of the Guru here? Anyone who
wants to sacrifice his life for the Sikh community? Anyone
with courage?" He hurled each sentence like a challenge.

The villagers felt very uncomfortable. The harangue had made them angry and they wanted to prove their manliness. At the same time Meet Singh's presence made them uneasy and they felt they were being disloyal to him.

"What are we supposed to do?" asked the lambardar plaintively.

"I will tell you what we are to do," answered the boy, pointing to himself. "If you have the courage to do it." He continued after a pause. "Tomorrow a trainload of Muslims is to cross the bridge to Pakistan. If you are men, this train should carry as many people dead to the other side as you have received."

A cold clammy feeling spread among the audience. People coughed nervously.

"The train will have Mano Majra Muslims on it," said Meet Singh without looking up.

"Bhai, you seem to know everything, don't you?" yelled the youth furiously. "Did you give them the tickets or is your son a Railway Babu? I don't know who the Muslims on the train are; I do not care. It is enough for me to know that they are Muslims. They will not cross this river alive. If you people agree with me, we can talk; if you are frightened, then say so and we will say 'Sat Sri Akal' to you and look for real men elsewhere."

Another long period of silence ensued. The lad beat a tattoo on his holster and patiently scanned the faces around him.

"There is a military guard at the bridge." It was Malli. He had been standing outside in the dark. He would not have dared to come back to Mano Majra alone. Yet there he was, boldly stepping into the gurdwara. Several members of his gang appeared at the door.

"You need not bother about the military or the police. No one will interfere. We will see to that," answered the lad looking back at him. "Are there any volunteers?"

"My life is at your disposal," said Malli heroically. The story of Jugga beating him had gone round the village. His reputation had to be redeemed.

"Bravo," said the speaker. "At least one man. The Guru asked for five lives when he made the Sikhs. Those Sikhs were supermen. We need many more than five. Who else is willing to lay down his life?"

Four of Malli's companions stepped over the threshold. They were followed by many others, mostly refugees. Some villagers who had only recently wept at the departure of their Muslim friends also stood up to volunteer. Each time anyone raised his hand the youth said "Bravo," and asked him to come and sit apart. More than fifty agreed to join in the escapade.

"That is enough," said the lad, raising his hand. "If I need any more volunteers, I will ask for them. Let us pray for the success of our venture."

Everyone stood up. Women put their children on the floor and joined the menfolk. The assembly faced the little cot on which the Granth lay wrapped, and folded their hands in prayer. The boy turned round to Meet Singh.

"Will you lead the prayer, Bhaiji?" he asked tauntingly.

"It is your mission, Sardar Sahib," replied Meet Singh humbly. "You lead the prayer."

The boy cleared his throat, shut his eyes and began to recite the names of the Gurus. He ended by asking for the Gurus' blessings for the venture. The assembly went down on their knees and rubbed their foreheads on the ground, loudly proclaiming:

> *In the name of Nanak,*
> *By the hope that faith doth instill,*
> *By the Grace of God,*
> *We bear the world nothing but good will.*

The crowd stood up again and began to chant:

> *The Sikhs will rule*
> *Their enemies will be scattered*
> *Only they that seek refuge will be saved!*

The little ceremonial ended with triumphant cries of "Sat

Sri Akal." Everyone sat down except the boy leader. The prayer had given him a veneer of humility. He joined his hands and apologized to the assembly.

"Sisters and brothers, forgive me for disturbing you at this late hour; you too, Bhaiji, and you, Lambardar Sahib, please forgive us for this inconvenience and for any angry words that I may have uttered; but this is in the service of the Guru. Volunteers will now adjourn to the other room; the others may rest. Sat Sri Akal."

"Sat Sri Akal," replied some of the audience.

Meet Singh's room on the side of the courtyard was cleared of women and children. The visitors moved in with the volunteers. More lamps were brought in. The leader spread out a map on one of the beds. He held up a hurricane lantern. The volunteers crowded round him to study the map.

"Can you all see the position of the bridge and the river from where you are?" he asked.

"Yes, yes," they answered impatiently.

"Have any of you got guns?"

They all looked at each other. No, no one had a gun.

"It does not matter," continued the leader. "We will have six or seven rifles, and probably a couple of sten guns as well. Bring your swords and spears. They will be more useful than guns." He paused.

"The plan is this. Tomorrow after sunset, when it is dark, we will stretch a rope across the first span of the bridge. It will be a foot above the height of the funnel of the engine. When the train passes under it, it will sweep off all the people sitting on the roof of the train. That will account for at least four to five hundred."

The eyes of the listeners sparkled with admiration. They nodded to each other and looked around. The lambardar and Meet Singh stood at the door listening. The boy turned round angrily:

153

"Bhaiji, what have you to do with this? Why don't you go and say your prayers?"

Both the lambardar and Meet Singh turned away sheepishly. The lambardar knew he too would be told off if he hung around.

"And you, Lambardar Sahib," said the boy. "You should be going to the police station to report."

Everyone laughed.

The boy silenced his audience by raising his hand. He continued: "The train is due to leave Chundunnugger after midnight. It will have no lights, not even on the engine. We will post people with flashlights along the track every hundred yards. Each one will give the signal to the next person as the train passes him. In any case, you will be able to hear it. People with swords and spears will be right at the bridge to deal with those that fall off the roof of the train. They will have to be killed and thrown into the river. Men with guns will be a few yards up the track and will shoot at the windows. There will be no danger of fire being returned. There are only a dozen Pakistani soldiers on the train. In the dark, they will not know where to shoot. They will not have time to load their guns. If they stop the train, we will take care of them and kill many more into the bargain."

It seemed a perfect plan, without the slightest danger of retaliation. Everyone was pleased.

"It is already past midnight," said the boy, folding up the map. "You'd all better get some sleep. Tomorrow morning we will go to the bridge and decide where each one is to be posted. The Sikhs are the chosen of God. Victory be to our God."

"Victory to our God," answered the others.

The meeting dispersed. Visitors found room in the gurdwara. So did Malli and his gang. Many of the villagers had gone away to their homes lest they get implicated in the crime by being present at the temple when the conspiracy was being hatched. The lambardar took two of the villagers with him and left for the police station at Chundunnugger.

"Well, Inspector Sahib, let them kill," said Hukum Chand wearily. "Let everyone kill. Just ask for help from other stations and keep a record of the messages you send. We must be able to prove that we did our best to stop them."

Hukum Chand looked a tired man. One week had aged him beyond recognition. The white at the roots of his hair had become longer. He had been shaving in a hurry and had cut himself in several places. His cheeks sagged and folds of flesh fell like dewlaps about his chin. He kept rubbing the corners of his eyes for the yellow which was not there.

"What am I to do?" he wailed. "The whole world has gone mad. Let it go mad! What does it matter if another thousand get killed? We will get a bulldozer and bury them as we did the others. We may not even need the bulldozer if this time it is going to be on the river. Just throw the corpses in the water. What is a few hundred out of four hundred million anyway? An epidemic takes ten times the number and no one even bothers."

The subinspector knew that this was not the real Hukum Chand. He was only trying to get the melancholia out of his system. The subinspector waited patiently, and then dropped a feeler.

"Yes, sir. I am keeping a record of all that is happening and what we are doing. Last evening, we had to evacuate Chundunnugger. I could not rely on the army nor my own constables. The best I could do was to ward off the attackers by telling them that Pakistan troops were in the town. That frightened them and I got the Muslims out in the nick of time. When the attackers discovered the trick, they looted and burned every Muslim house they could. I believe some of them planned to come to the police station for me, but better counsel prevailed. So you see, sir, all I got was abuse from the Muslims for evicting them from their homes; abuse from the Sikhs for having robbed them of the loot they were expecting. Now I suppose the government will also abuse me for something or other. All I really have is my big thumb." The subinspector stuck out his thumb and smiled.

Hukum Chand's mind was not itself that morning. He did not seem to realize the full import of the subinspector's report.

"Yes, Inspector Sahib, you and I are going to get nothing out of this except a bad name. What can we do? Everyone has gone trigger-happy. People empty their rifle magazines into densely packed trains, motor convoys, columns of marching refugees, as if they were squirting red water at the Holi festival; it is a bloody Holi. What sense is there in going to a place where bullets fly? The bullet does not pause and consider 'This is Hukum Chand, I must not touch him.' Nor does a bullet have a name written on it saying 'Sent by So-and-so.' Even if it did bear a name—once inside, what consolation would it be to us to know who fired it? No, Inspector Sahib, the only thing a sane person can do in a lunatic asylum is to pretend that he is as mad as the others and at the first opportunity scale the walls and get out."

The subinspector was used to these sermons and knew how little they represented the magistrate's real self. But Hukum Chand's apparent inability to take a hint was surprising. He was known for never saying a thing straight; he considered it stupid. To him the art of diplomacy was to state a simple thing in an involved manner. It never got one into trouble. It could never be quoted as having implied this or that. At the same time, it gave one the reputation of being shrewd and clever. Hukum Chand was as adept at discovering innuendoes as he was at making them. This morning he seemed to be giving his mind a rest.

"You should have been in Chundunnugger yesterday," said the subinspector, bringing the conversation back to the actual problem which faced him. "If I had been five minutes later, there would not have been one Muslim left alive. As it is, not one was killed. I was able to take them all out."

The subinspector emphasized "not one" and "all." He watched Hukum Chand's reaction.

It worked. Hukum Chand stopped rubbing the corners of his eyes and asked casually, as if he were only seeking information, "You mean to tell me there is not one Muslim family left in Chundunnugger?"

"No, sir, not one."

"I suppose," said Hukum Chand, clearing his throat, "they will come back when all this blows over?"

"Maybe," the subinspector answered. "There is not much for them to come back to. Their homes have been burned or occupied. And if anyone did come back his or her life would not be worth the tiniest shell in the sea."

"It will not last forever. You see how things change. Within a week they will be back in Chundunnugger and the Sikhs and Muslims will be drinking water out of the same pitcher." Hukum Chand detected the note of false hope in his own voice. So did the subinspector.

"You may be right, sir. But it will certainly take more than a week for that to happen. Chundunnugger refugees are being taken to Pakistan by train tonight. God alone knows how many will go across the bridge alive; those that do are not likely to want to come back in a hurry."

The subinspector had hit the mark. Hukum Chand's face went pale. He could no longer keep up the pretense.

"How do you know that Chundunnugger refugees are going by the night train?" he asked.

"I got it from the camp commander. There was danger of attack on the camp itself, so he decided to get the first train available to take the refugees out. If they do not go, probably no one will be left alive. If they do, some at least may get through, if the train is running at some speed. They are not planning to derail the train; they want it to go on to Pakistan with a cargo of corpses."

Hukum Chand clutched the arms of his chair convulsively.

"Why don't you warn the camp commander about it? He may decide not to go."

"Cherisher of the poor," explained the subinspector patiently, "I have not told him anything about the proposed attack on the train because if he does not go the whole camp may be destroyed. There are mobs of twenty to thirty thousand armed villagers thirsting for blood. I have fifty policemen with me and not one of them would fire a shot at a Sikh. But if your honor can use influence with these mobs, I can tell the camp commander about the plans to ambush the train and persuade him not to go."

The subinspector was hitting below the belt.

"No, no," stuttered the magistrate. "What can influence do with armed mobs? No. We must think."

Hukum Chand sank back in his chair. He covered his face with his hands. He beat his forehead gently with his clenched fist. He tugged at his hair as if he could pull ideas out of his brain.

"What has happened to those two men you arrested for the moneylender's murder?" he asked after some time.

The subinspector did not see the relevance of the inquiry.

"They are still in the lockup. You ordered me to keep them till the trouble was over. At this rate it seems I will have to keep them for some months."

"Are there any Muslim females, or any stray Muslims who have refused to leave Mano Majra?"

"No, sir, not one remains. Men, women, children, all have left," answered the subinspector. He was still unable to catch up with Hukum Chand's train of thought.

"What about Jugga's weaver girl you told me about? What was her name?"

"Nooran."

"Ah yes, Nooran. Where is she?"

"She has left. Her father was a sort of leader of the Muslims of Mano Majra. The lambardar told me a great deal about him. He had just one child, this girl Nooran; she is the one alleged to be carrying on with the dacoit Jugga."

"And tnis other fellow, didn't you say he was a political worker of some sort?"

"Yes, sir. People's Party or something like that. I think he is a Muslim Leaguer masquerading under a false label. I examined . . . "

"Have you got any blank official papers for orders?" cut in Hukum Chand impatiently.

"Yes, sir," answered the subinspector. He fished out several pieces of yellow printed paper and handed them to the magistrate.

Hukum Chand stretched out his hand and plucked the subinspector's fountain pen from his pocket.

"What are the names of the prisoners?" he asked, spreading out the sheets on the table.

"Jugga budmash and . . ."

"Jugga budmash," interrupted Hukum Chand, filling in a blank and signing it. "Jugga budmash, and . . . ?" he asked taking the other paper.

"Iqbal Mohammed or Mohammed Iqbal. I am not sure which."

"Not Iqbal Mohammed, Inspector Sahib. Nor Mohammed Iqbal. Iqbal Singh," he said, writing with a flourish. The subinspector looked a little stupefied. How did Hukum Chand know? Had Meet Singh been around calling on the magistrate?

"Sir, you should not believe everyone. I examined . . . "

"Do you really believe an educated Muslim would dare to come to these parts in times like these? Do you think any party would be so foolish as to send a Muslim to preach peace to Sikh peasants thirsting for Muslim blood, Inspector Sahib? Where is your imagination?"

The subinspector was subdued. It did seem unlikely that an

educated man would risk his neck for any cause. Besides, he had noticed on Iqbal's right wrist the steel bangle all Sikhs wear.

"Your honor must be right, but what has this to do with the preventing of an attack on the train?"

"My honor *is* right," said Hukum Chand triumphantly. "And you will soon know why. Think about it on your way to Chundunnugger. As soon as you get there release both the men and see that they leave for Mano Majra immediately. If necessary, get them a tonga. They must be in the village by the evening."

The subinspector took the papers, and saluted. He sped back to the police station on his cycle. Gradually the clouds of confusion lifted from his mind. Hukum Chand's plan became as crystal clear as a day after heavy rain.

"You will find Mano Majra somewhat changed," the subinspector remarked, casually addressing the table in front of him. Iqbal and Jugga stood facing him on the other side.

"Why don't you sit down, Babu Sahib?" said the subinspector. This time he spoke directly to Iqbal. "Please take a chair. Oi, what is your name? Why don't you bring a chair for the Babu Sahib?" he shouted at a constable. "I know you are angry with me, but it is not my fault," he continued. "I have my duty to do. You as an educated man know what would happen if I were to treat people differently."

The constable brought a chair for Iqbal.

"Do sit down. Shall I get you a cup of tea or something before you go?" The subinspector smiled unctuously.

"It is very kind of you. I would rather keep standing; I have been sitting in the cell all these days. If you do not mind, I would like to leave as soon as you have finished with the formalities," answered Iqbal without responding to the other's smile.

"You are free to go whenever and wherever you want to go. I have sent for a tonga to take you to Mano Majra. I will send an armed constable to accompany you. It is not safe to be about in Chundunnugger or to travel unescorted."

The subinspector picked up a yellow paper and read: "Juggut Singh, son of Alam Singh, age twenty-four, caste Sikh of village Mano Majra, budmash number ten."

"Yes, sir," interrupted Jugga, smiling. The treatment he had received from the police had not made any difference to him. His equation with authority was simple: he was on the other side. Personalities did not come into it. Subinspectors and policemen were people in khaki who frequently arrested him, always abused him, and sometimes beat him. Since they abused and beat him without anger or hate, they were not human beings with names. They were only denominations one tried to get the better of. If one failed, it was just bad luck.

"You are being released, but you must appear before Mr. Hukum Chand, Deputy Commissioner, on the first of October 1947, at ten a.m. Put your thumb impression on this."

The subinspector opened a flat tin box with a black gauze padding inside it. He caught Juggut Singh's thumb in his hand, rubbed it on the damp pad and pressed it on the paper.

"Have I permission to go?" asked Jugga.

"You can go with Babu Sahib in the tonga; otherwise you will not get home before dark." He looked up at Jugga and repeated slowly, "You will not find Mano Majra the same."

Neither of the men showed any interest in the subinspector's remark about Mano Majra. The subinspector spread out another piece of paper and read: "Mr. Iqbal Singh, social worker."

Iqbal looked at the paper cynically.

"Not Mohammed Iqbal, member of the Muslim League? You seem to fabricate facts and documents as it pleases you."

The subinspector grinned. "Everyone makes mistakes. To err is human, to forgive divine," he added in English. "I admit my mistake."

"That is very generous of you," answered Iqbal. "I had always believed that the Indian Police were infallible."

"You can make fun of me if you like; you do not realize that if you had been going about lecturing as you intended and had fallen into the hands of a Sikh mob, they would not have listened to your arguments. They would have stripped you to find out whether or not you were circumcised. That is the only test they have these days for a person who has not got long hair and a beard. Then they kill. You should be grateful to me."

Iqbal was in no mood to talk. Besides, the subject was not one he wanted to discuss with anyone. He resented the way the subinspector took the liberty of mentioning it.

"You will find big changes in Mano Majra!" warned the subinspector for the third time; neither Jugga nor Iqbal showed any response. Iqbal laid down on the table the book he had been holding and turned away without a word of thanks or farewell. Jugga felt the floor with his feet for his shoes.

"All Mussulmans have gone from Mano Majra," said the subinspector dramatically.

Jugga stopped shuffling his feet. "Where have they gone?"

"Yesterday they were taken to the refugee camp. Tonight they will go by train to Pakistan."

"Was there any trouble in the village, Inspector Sahib? Why did they have to go?"

"There would have been if they had not gone. There are lots of outsiders going about with guns killing Muslims; Malli and his men have joined them. If the Muslims had not left Mano Majra, Malli would have finished them off by now. He has taken all their things—cows, buffaloes, oxen, mares, chickens, utensils. Malli has done well."

Jugga's temper shot up at once. "That penis of a pig who sleeps with his mother, pimps for his sister and daughter, if he puts his foot in Mano Majra I will stick my bamboo pole up his behind!"

The subinspector pursed his lips in a taunting smile. "You talk big, Sardara. Just because you caught him unawares by his hair and beat him, you think you are a lion. Malli is not a woman with henna on his palms or bangles on his wrists. He has been in Mano Majra and taken all the things he wanted; he is still there. You will see him when you get back."

"He will run like a jackal when he hears my name."

"Men of his gang are with him. So are many others, all armed with guns and pistols. You had better behave sensibly if you hold your life dear."

Jugga nodded his head. "Right, Inspector Sahib. We will meet again. Then ask me about Malli." His temper got the better of him. "If I do not spit in his bottom, my name is not Juggut Singh." He rubbed his mouth with the back of his hand. "If I do not spit in Malli's mouth, my name is not Juggut Singh." This time Juggut Singh spat on his own hand and rubbed it on his thigh. His temper rose to fever heat. "If it had not been for your policemen in their uniforms, I would like to meet the father of a son who could dare to bat an eyelid before Juggut Singh," he added, throwing out his chest.

"All right, all right, Sardar Juggut Singh, we agree you are a big brave man. At least you think so," smiled the subinspector. "You had better get home before dark. Take the Babu Sahib with you. Babu Sahib, you need have no fear. You have the district's bravest man to look after you."

Before Juggut Singh could reply to the subinspector's sarcasm, a constable came in to announce that he had got a tonga.

"Sat Sri Akal, Inspector Sahib. When Malli comes crying to lodge a report against me, then you will believe that Juggut Singh is not a man of hollow words."

The subinspector laughed. "Sat Sri Akal, Juggut Singha. Sat Sri Akal, Iqbal Singhji."

Iqbal walked away without turning back.

The tonga left Chundunnugger in the afternoon. It was a long uneventful journey. This time Jugga sat on the front seat with the policeman and the driver, leaving the rear seat all to Iqbal.

163

No one was in a mood to talk. Bhola, the driver, had been pressed into service by the police at a time when it was not safe to step out of the house. He took it out on his skinny brown horse, whipping and swearing continuously. The others were absorbed in their own thoughts.

The countryside also was still. There were large expanses of water which made it look flatter than usual. There were no men or women in the fields. Not even cattle grazing. The two villages they passed seemed deserted except for the dogs. Once or twice they caught a fleeting glimpse of someone stepping behind a wall or peering round a corner—and that someone carried a gun or a spear.

Iqbal realized that it was the company of Jugga and the constable, who were known Sikhs, that really saved him from being stopped and questioned. He wished he could get out of this place where he had to prove his Sikhism to save his life. He would pick up his things from Mano Majra and catch the first train. Perhaps there were no trains. And if there were, could he risk getting onto one? He cursed his luck for having a name like Iqbal, and then for being a . . . Where on earth except in India would a man's life depend on whether or not his foreskin had been removed? It would be laughable if it were not tragic. He would have to stay in Mano Majra for several days and stay close to Meet Singh for protection—Meet Singh with his unkempt appearance and two trips a day to the fields to defecate. The thought was revolting. If only he could get out to Delhi and to civilization! He would report on his arrest; the party paper would frontpage the news with his photograph: *ANGLO-AMERICAN CAPITALIST CONSPIRACY TO CREATE CHAOS* (lovely alliteration). *COMRADE IQBAL IMPRISONED ON BORDER.* It would all go to make him a hero.

Jugga's immediate concern was the fate of Nooran. He did not look at his companions in the tonga or at the villages. He had forgotten about Malli. At the back of his mind persisted a feeling that Nooran would be in Mano Majra. No one could have wanted Imam Baksh to go. Even if he had left with the other Muslims, Nooran would be hiding somewhere in the fields, or would have come to his mother. He hoped his mother had not turned her out. If she had, he would let her have it. He would walk out and never come back. She would spend the rest of her days regretting having done it.

Jugga was lost in his thoughts, concerned and angry alternately, when the tonga slowed down to pass through the lane to the Sikh temple. He jumped off the moving vehicle and disappeared into the darkness without a word of farewell.

Iqbal stepped off the tonga and stretched his limbs. The driver and the constable had a whispered consultation.

"Can I be of any more service to you, Babu Sahib?" asked the policeman.

"No. No, thank you. I am all right. It is very kind of you." Iqbal did not like the prospect of going into the gurdwara alone, but he could not bring himself to ask the others to come with him.

"Babuji, we have a long way to go. My horse has been out all day without any food or water; and you know the times."

"Yes, you can go back. Thank you. Sat Sri Akal."

"Sat Sri Akal."

The courtyard of the gurdwara was spotted with rings of light cast by hurricane lamps and fires on improvised hearths over which women were cooking the evening meal. Inside the main hall was a circle of people around Meet Singh, who was reciting the evening prayer. The room in which Iqbal had left his things was locked.

Iqbal took off his shoes, covered his head with a handkerchief and joined the gathering. Some people shifted to make room for him. Iqbal noticed people looking at him and whispering to each other. Most of them were old men dressed like town folk. It was quite obvious that they were refugees.

When the prayer was over, Meet Singh wrapped the massive volume in velvet and laid it to rest on the cot on which it had been lying open. He spoke to Iqbal before anyone else could start asking questions.

"Sat Sri Akal, Iqbal Singhji. I am glad you are back. You must be hungry."

Iqbal realized that Meet Singh had deliberately mentioned his surname. He could feel the tension relax. Some of the men turned around and said "Sat Sri Akal."

"Sat Sri Akal," answered Iqbal and got up to join Meet Singh.

"Sardar Iqbal Singh," said Meet Singh, introducing him to the others, "is a social worker. He has been in England for many years."

A host of admiring eyes were turned on Iqbal, "the England-returned." The "Sat Sri Akal"'s were repeated. Iqbal felt embarrassed.

"You are a Sikh, Iqbal Singhji?" inquired one of the men.

"Yes." A fortnight earlier he would have replied emphatically "No," or "I have no religion" or "Religion is irrelevant." The situation was different now, and in any case it was true that he was born a Sikh.

"Was it in England you cut your hair?" asked the same person.

"No, sir," answered Iqbal, completely confused. "I never grew my hair long. I am just a Sikh without long hair and beard."

"Your parents must have been unorthodox," said Meet Singh coming to his aid. The statement allayed suspicion but left Iqbal with an uneasy conscience.

Meet Singh fumbled with the cord of his shorts and pulled up a bunch of keys dangling at the end. He picked up the hurricane lantern from the stool beside the scriptures and led the way through the courtyard to the room.

"I kept your things locked in the room. You can take them. I will get you some food."

"No, Bhaiji, do not bother. I have enough with me. Tell me,

what has happened in the village since I left? Who are all these people?"

The bhai unlocked the door and lit an oil lamp in the niche. Iqbal opened his kit bag and emptied its contents on a charpoy. There were several copper-gold tins of fish paste, butter and cheese; aluminum forks, knives and spoons, and celluloid cups and saucers.

"Bhaiji, what has been happening?" Iqbal asked again.

"What has been happening? Ask me what has not been happening. Trainloads of dead people came to Mano Majra. We burned one lot and buried another. The river was flooded with corpses. Muslims were evacuated, and in their place, refugees have come from Pakistan. What more do you want to know?"

Iqbal wiped a celluloid plate and tumbler with his handkerchief. He fished out his silver hip flask and shook it. It was full.

"What have you in that silver bottle?"

"Oh this? Medicine," faltered Iqbal. "It gives me an appetite for food," he added with a smile.

"And then you take pills to digest it?"

Iqbal laughed. "Yes, and more to make the bowels work. Tell me, was there any killing in the village?"

"No," said the bhai casually. He was more interested in watching Iqbal inflating the air mattress. "But there will be. Is it nice sleeping on this? Does everyone in England sleep on these?"

"What do you mean—there will be killing?" asked Iqbal, plugging the end of the mattress. "All Muslims have left, haven't they?"

"Yes, but they are going to attack the train near the bridge tonight. It is taking Muslims of Chundunnugger and Mano Majra to Pakistan. Your pillow is also full of air."

"Yes. Who are they? Not the villagers?"

"I do not know all of them. Some people in uniforms came in military cars. They had pistols and guns. The refugees have joined them. So have Malli budmash and his gang—and some

167

villagers. Wouldn't this burst if a heavy person slept on it?" asked Meet Singh, tapping the mattress.

"I see," said Iqbal, ignoring Meet Singh's question. "I see the trick now. That is why the police released Malli. Now I suppose Jugga will join them, too. It is all arranged." He stretched himself on the mattress and tucked the pillow under his armpit. "Bhaiji, can't you stop it? They all listen to you."

Meet Singh patted and smoothed the air mattress and sat down on the floor.

"Who listens to an old bhai? These are bad times, Iqbal Singhji, very bad times. There is no faith or religion. All one can do is to crouch in a safe corner till the storm blows over. This would not do for a newly married couple," he added, slapping the mattress affectionately.

Iqbal was agitated. "You cannot let this sort of thing happen! Can't you tell them that the people on the train are the very same people they were addressing as uncles, aunts, brothers and sisters?"

Meet Singh sighed. He wiped a tear with the scarf on his shoulder.

"What difference will my telling them make? They know what they are doing. They will kill. If it is a success, they will come to the gurdwara for thanksgiving. They will also make offerings to wash away their sins. Iqbal Singhji, tell me about yourself. Have you been well? Did they treat you properly at the police station?"

"Yes, yes, I was all right," snapped Iqbal impatiently. "Why don't you do something? You must!"

"I have done all I could. My duty is to tell people what is right and what is not. If they insist on doing evil, I ask God to forgive them. I can only pray; the rest is for the police and the magistrates. And for you."

"Me? Why me?" asked Iqbal with a startled innocence. "What have I to do with it? I do not know these people. Why should they listen to a stranger?"

"When you came you were going to speak to them about something. Why don't you tell them now?"

Iqbal felt cornered. "Bhaiji, when people go about with guns and spears you can only talk back with guns and spears. If you cannot do that, then it is best to keep out of their way."

"That is exactly what I say. I thought you with your European ideas had some other remedy. Let me get you some hot spinach. I have just cooked it," added Meet Singh getting up.

"No, no, Bhaiji, I have all I want in my tins. If I want something I will ask you for it. I have a little work to do before I eat."

Meet Singh put the hurricane lantern on a stool by the bed and went back to the hall.

Iqbal put his plates, knife, fork, and tins back into the haversack. He felt a little feverish, the sort of feverishness one feels when one is about to make a declaration of love. It was time for a declaration of something. Only he was not sure what it should be.

Should he go out, face the mob and tell them in clear ringing tones that this was wrong—immoral? Walk right up to them with his eyes fixing the armed crowd in a frame—without flinching, without turning, like the heroes on the screen who become bigger and bigger as they walk right into the camera. Then with dignity fall under a volley of blows, or preferably a volley of rifleshots. A cold thrill went down Iqbal's spine.

There would be no one to see this supreme act of sacrifice. They would kill him just as they would kill the others. He was not neutral in their eyes. They would just strip him and see. Circumcised, therefore Muslim. It would be an utter waste of life! And what would it gain? A few subhuman species were going to slaughter some of their own kind—a mild setback to the annual increase of four million. It was not as if you were going to save good people from bad. If the others had the chance, they would do as much. In fact they were doing so, just a little beyond the river. It was pointless. In a state of chaos self-preservation is the supreme duty.

Iqbal unscrewed the top of his hip flask and poured out a large whisky in a celluloid tumbler. He gulped it down neat.

When bullets fly about, what is the point of sticking out your head and getting shot? The bullet is neutral. It hits the good and the bad, the important and the insignificant, without distinction. If there were people to see the act of self-immolation, as on a cinema screen, the sacrifice might be worth while: a moral lesson might be conveyed. If all that was likely to happen was that next morning your corpse would be found among thousands of others, looking just like them—cropped hair, shaven chin . . . even circumcised—who would know that you were not a Muslim victim of a massacre? Who would know that you were a Sikh who, with full knowledge of the consequences, had walked into the face of a firing squad to prove that it was important that good should triumph over evil? And God—no, not God; He was irrelevant.

Iqbal poured another whisky. It seemed to sharpen his mind.

The point of sacrifice, he thought, is the purpose. For the purpose, it is not enough that a thing is intrinsically good: it must be known to be good. It is not enough only to know within one's self that one is in the right: the satisfaction would be posthumous. This was not the same thing as taking punishment at school to save some friend. In that case you could feel good and live to enjoy the sacrifice; in this one you were going to be killed. It would do no good to society: society would never know. Nor to yourself: you would be dead. That figure on the screen, facing thousands of people who looked tense and concerned! They were ready to receive the lesson. That was the crux of the whole thing. The doer must do only when the receiver is ready to receive. Otherwise, the act is wasted.

He filled the glass again. Everything was becoming clearer.

If you really believe that things are so rotten that your first duty is to destroy—to wipe the slate clean—then you should not turn green at small acts of destruction. Your duty is to connive with those who make the conflagration, not to turn a moral hose-pipe on them—to create such a mighty chaos that all that is rotten like selfishness, intolerance, greed, falsehood, sycophancy, is drowned. In blood, if necessary.

India is constipated with a lot of humbug. Take religion. For the Hindu, it means little besides caste and cow-protection. For the Muslim, circumcision and kosher meat. For the Sikh, long hair and hatred of the Muslim. For the Christian, Hinduism with a sola topee. For the Parsi, fire-worship and feeding vultures. Ethics, which should be the kernel of a religious code, has been carefully removed. Take philosophy, about which there is so much hoo-ha. It is just muddleheadedness masquerading as mysticism. And Yoga, particularly Yoga, that excellent earner of dollars! Stand on your head. Sit cross-legged and tickle your navel with your nose. Have perfect control over the senses. Make women come till they cry "Enough!" and you can say "Next, please" without opening your eyes. And all the mumbo-jumbo of reincarnation. Man into ox into ape into beetle into eight million four hundred thousand kinds of animate things. Proof? We do not go in for such pedestrian pastimes as proof! That is Western. We are of the mysterious East. No proof, just faith. No reason; just faith. Thought, which should be the sine qua non of a philosophical code, is dispensed with. We climb to sublime heights on the wings of fancy. We do the rope trick in all spheres of creative life. As long as the world credulously believes in our capacity to make a rope rise skyward and a little boy climb it till he is out of view, so long will our brand of humbug thrive.

Take art and music. Why has contemporary Indian painting, music, architecture and sculpture been such a flop? Because it keeps harking back to B. C. Harking back would be all right if it did not become a pattern—a deadweight. If it does, then we are in a cul-de-sac of art forms. We explain the unattractive by pretending it is esoteric. Or we break out altogether—like modern Indian music of the films. It is all tango and rhumba or samba played on Hawaiian guitars, violins, accordions and clarinets. It is ugly. It must be scrapped like the rest.

He wasn't quite sure what he meant. He poured another whisky.

Consciousness of the bad is an essential prerequisite to the promotion of the good. It is no use trying to build a second story on a house whose walls are rotten. It is best to demolish it. It is both cowardly and foolhardy to kowtow to social standards when one believes neither in the society nor in its standards. Their courage is your cowardice, their cowardice your courage. It is all a matter of nomenclature. One could say it needs courage to be a coward. A conundrum, but a quotable one. Make a note of it.

And have another whisky. The whisky was like water. It had no taste. Iqbal shook the flask. He heard a faint splashing. It wasn't empty. Thank God, it wasn't empty.

If you look at things as they are, he told himself, there does not seem to be a code either of man or of God on which one can pattern one's conduct. Wrong triumphs over right as much as right over wrong. Sometimes its triumphs are greater. What happens ultimately, you do not know. In such circumstances what can you do but cultivate an utter indifference to all values? Nothing matters. Nothing whatever . . .

Iqbal fell asleep, with the celluloid glass in his hand and the lamp burning on the stool beside him.

In the courtyard of the gurdwara, the fires on the hearths had burned to ashes. A gust of wind occasionally fanned a glowing ember. Lamps had been dimmed. Men, women and children lay sprawled about on the floor of the main room. Meet Singh was awake. He was sweeping the floor and tidying up the mess.

Somebody started banging at the door with his fists. Meet

Singh stopped sweeping and went across the courtyard muttering, "Who is it?"

He undid the latch. Jugga stepped inside. In the dark he looked larger than ever. His figure filled the doorway.

"Why, Juggut Singhji, what business have you here at this hour?" asked Meet Singh.

"Bhai," he whispered, "I want the Guru's word. Will you read me a verse?"

"I have laid the Granth Sahib to rest for the night," Meet Sing said. "What is it that you want to do?"

"It does not matter about that," said Jugga impatiently. He put a heavy hand on Meet Singh's shoulder. "Will you just read me a few lines quickly?"

Meet Singh led the way, grumbling. "You never came to the gurdwara any other time. Now when the scripture is resting and people are asleep, you want me to read the Guru's word. It is not proper. I will read you a piece from the Morning Prayer."

"It does not matter what you read. Just read it."

Meet Singh turned up the wick of one of the lanterns. Its sooty chimney became bright. He sat down beside the cot on which the scripture lay. Jugga picked up the fly whisk from beneath the cot and began waving it over Meet Singh's head. Meet Singh got out a small prayer book, put it to his forehead and began to read the verse on the page which he happened to have opened to:

He who made the night and day,
The days of the week and the seasons.
He who made the breezes blow, the waters run,
The fires and the lower regions.
Made the earth—the temple of law.
He who made creatures of diverse kinds
With a multitude of names,
Made this the law—
By thought and deed be judged forsooth,

> For God is True and dispenseth Truth.
> There the elect his court adorn,
> And God Himself their actions honors.
> There are sorted deeds that were done and bore fruit,
> From those that to action could never ripen.
> This, O Nanak, shall hereafter happen.

Meet Singh shut the prayer book and again put it to his forehead. He began to mumble the epilogue to the morning prayer:

> Air, water and earth,
> Of these are we made,
> Air like the Guru's word gives the breath of life
> To the babe born of the great mother Earth
> Sired by the waters.

His voice tapered off to an inaudible whisper. Juggut Singh put back the fly whisk and rubbed his forehead on the ground in front of the scripture.

"Is that good?" he asked naively.

"All the Guru's word is good," answered Meet Singh solemnly.

"What does it mean?"

"What have you to do with meaning? It is just the Guru's word. If you are going to do something good, the Guru will help you; if you are going to do something bad, the Guru will stand in your way. If you persist in doing it, he will punish you till you repent, and then forgive you."

"Yes, what will I do with the meaning? All right, Bhaiji. Sat Sri Akal."

"Sat Sri Akal."

Jugga rubbed his forehead on the ground again and got up. He threaded his way through the sleeping assembly and picked up his shoes. There was a light in one of the rooms. Jugga looked in. He recognized the head with tousled hair on the pillow. Iqbal was sleeping with the silver hip flask lying on his chest.

"Sat Sri Akal, Babuji," he said softly. There was no reply. "Are you asleep?"

"Do not disturb him," interrupted Meet Singh in a whisper. "He is not feeling well. He has been taking medicine to sleep."

"Acha, Bhaiji, you say 'Sat Sri Akal to him for me." Juggut Singh went out of the gurdwara.

"No fool like an old fool." The sentence kept recurring in Hukum Chand's mind. He tried to dismiss it, but it came back again and again: "No fool like an old fool." It was bad enough for a married man in his fifties to go picking up women. To get emotionally involved with a girl young enough to be his daughter and a Muslim prostitute at that! That was *too* ludicrous. He must be losing his grip on things. He was getting senile and stupid.

The feeling of elation which his plan had given him in the morning was gone. Instead there was one of anxiety, uncertainty and old age. He had released the budmash and the social worker without knowing much about them. They probably had no more nerve than he. Some of the leftist social workers were known to be a daring lot. This one, however, was an intellectual, the sort people contemptuously describe as the armchair variety. He would probably do nothing except criticize others for failing to do their duty. The budmash was a notorious daredevil. He had been in train robberies, car holdups, dacoities and murders. It was money he was after, or revenge. The only chance of his doing anything was to settle scores with Malli. If Malli had fled when he heard of Jugga's arrival, Jugga would lose interest and might even join the gang in killing and looting the victims of the ambush. His type never risked their necks for women. If Nooran was killed, he would pick up another girl.

Hukum Chand was also uneasy about his own role. Was it enough to get others to do the work for him? Magistrates were responsible for maintenance of law and order. But they maintained order with power behind them; not opposing them. Where was the power? What were the people in Delhi doing? Making fine speeches in the assembly! Loud-speakers magnifying their egos; lovely-looking foreign women in the visitors' galleries in breathless admiration. "He is a great man, this Mr. Nehru of yours. I do think he is the greatest man in the world today. And how handsome! Wasn't that a wonderful thing to say? 'Long ago we made a tryst with destiny and now the time comes when we shall redeem our pledge, not wholly or in full measure but very substantially.'" Yes, Mr. Prime Minister, you made your tryst. So did many others.

There was Hukum Chand's colleague Prem Singh who went back to fetch his wife's jewelry from Lahore. He made his tryst at Faletti's Hotel where European sahibs used to flirt with each other's wives. It is next door to the Punjab Assembly building where Pakistani parliamentarians talked democracy and made laws. Prem Singh whiled away time drinking beer and offering it to the Englishmen staying in the hotel. Over the privet hedge a dozen heads with fez caps and Pathan turbans waited for him. He drank more beer and forced it on his English friends and on the orchestra. His dates across the hedge waited patiently. The Englishmen drank a lot of beer and whisky and said Prem Singh was a grand chap. But it was late for dinner so they said "Good night Mr. . . . Did not catch your name. Yes, of course, Mr. Singh. Thank you very much, Mr. Singh. See you again." . . . "Nice old Wog. Can hold his drink too," they said in the dining room. Even the orchestra had more beer than ever before. "What would you like us to play, sir?" asked Mendoza the Goan band leader. "It is rather late and we must close down now." Prem Singh did not know the name of any European piece of music. He thought hard. He remembered one of the Englishmen had asked for something which sounded like "bananas." "Bananas," said Prem Singh. "'We'll Have No Bananas Today.' Yes, sir." Mendoza, DeMello, DeSilva, De-Saram and Gomes strummed "Bananas." Prem Singh walked across the lawn to the gate. His dates also moved along the hedge to the gate. The band saw Prem Singh leave so they switched onto "God Save the King."

There was Sundari, the daughter of Hukum Chand's orderly. She had made her tryst with destiny on the road to Gujranwala. She had been married four days and both her arms were covered with red lacquer bangles and the henna on her palms was still a deep vermilion. She had not yet slept with Mansa Ram. Their relatives had not left them alone for a minute. She had hardly seen his face through her veil. Now he was taking her to Gujranwala where he worked as a peon and had a little room of his own in the Sessions Court compound. There would be no relatives and he would certainly try it. He did not seem particularly keen, sitting in the bus talking loudly to all the other passengers. Men often pretended indifference. No one would really believe that she wanted him either—what with the veil across her face and not a word! "Do not take any of the lacquer bangles off. It brings bad luck," her girl friends had said to her. "Let him break them when he makes love to you and mauls you." There were a dozen on each of her arms, covering them from the wrists to the elbows. She felt them with her fingers. They were hard and brittle. He would have to do a lot of hugging and savaging to break them. She stopped daydreaming as the bus pulled up. There were large stones on the road. Then hundreds of people surrounded them. Everyone was ordered off the bus. Sikhs were just hacked to death. The clean-shaven were stripped. Those that were circumcised were forgiven. Those that were not, were circumcised. Not just the foreskin: the whole thing was cut off. She who had not really had a good look at Mansa Ram was shown her husband completely naked. They held him by the arms and legs and one man cut off his penis and gave it to her. The mob made love to her. She did not have to take off any one of her bangles. They were all smashed as she lay in the road, being taken by one man and another and another. That should have brought her a lot of good luck!

Sunder Singh's case was different. Hukum Chand had had

177

him recruited for the army. He had done well. He was a big, brave Sikh with a row of medals won in battles in Burma, Eritrea and Italy. The government had given him land in Sindh. He came to his tryst by train, along with his wife and three children. There were over five hundred men and women in a compartment meant to carry "40 sitting, 12 sleeping." There was just one little lavatory in the corner without any water in the cistern. It was 115° in the shade; but there was no shade—not a shrub within miles. Only the sun and the sand . . . and no water. At all stations there were people with spears along the railings. Then the train was held up at a station for four days. No one was allowed to get off. Sunder Singh's children cried for water and food. So did everyone else. Sunder Singh gave them his urine to drink. Then that dried up too. So he pulled out his revolver and shot them all. Shangara Singh aged six with his long brown-blonde hair tied up in a topknot, Deepo aged four with curling eyelashes, and Amro, four months old, who tugged at her mother's dry breasts with her gums and puckered up her face till it was full of wrinkles, crying frantically. Sunder Singh also shot his wife. Then he lost his nerve. He put the revolver to his temple but did not fire. There was no point in killing himself. The train had begun to move. He heaved out the corpses of his wife and children and came along to India. He did not redeem the pledge. Only his family did.

Hukum Chand felt wretched. The night had fallen. Frogs called from the river. Fireflies twinkled about the jasmines near the verandah. The bearer had brought whisky and Hukum Chand had sent it away. The bearer had laid out the dinner but he had not touched the food. He had the lamp removed and sat alone in the dark, staring into space.

Why had he let the girl go back to Chundunnugger? Why? he asked himself, hitting his forehead with his fist. If only she were here in the rest house with him, he would not bother if the rest of the world went to hell. But she was not here; she was in the train. He could hear its rumble.

Hukum Chand slid off his chair, covered his face with his arms and started to cry. Then he raised his face to the sky and began to pray.

A little after eleven, the moon came up. It looked tired and dissipated. It flooded the plain with a weary pale light in which everything was a little blurred. Near the bridge there was very little moonlight. The high railway embankment cast a wall of dark shadow.

Sandbags, which had guarded the machine-gun nest near the signal, were littered about on either side of the railway tracks. The signal scaffolding stood like an enormous sentry watching over the scene. Two large oval eyes, one on top of the other, glowed red. The two hands of the signal stood stiffly parallel to each other. The bushes along the bank looked like a jungle. The river did not glisten; it was like a sheet of slate with just a suspicion of a ripple here and there.

A good distance from the embankment, behind a thick cluster of pampas, was a jeep with its engine purring gently. There was no one in it. The men had spread themselves on either side of the railway line a few feet from each other. They sat on their haunches with their rifles and spears between their legs. On the first steel span of the bridge a thick rope was tied horizontally above the railway line. It was about twenty feet above the track.

It was too dark for the men to recognize each other. So they talked loudly. Then somebody called.

"Silence! Listen!"

They listened. It was nothing. Only the wind in the reeds.

"Silence anyhow," came the command of the leader. "If you talk like this, you will not hear the train in time."

They began to talk in whispers.

There was a shimmy-shammy noise of trembling steel wires as one of the signals came down. Its oval eye changed from red to a bright green. The whispering stopped. The men got up and took their positions ten yards away from the track.

There was a steady rumbling sound punctuated by soft puff-puffs. A man ran up to the line and put his ear on the steel rail.

"Come back, you fool," yelled the leader in a hoarse whisper.

"It is the train," he announced triumphantly.

"Get back!" repeated the leader fiercely.

All eyes strained toward the gray space where the rumbling of the train came from. Then they shifted to the rope, stiff as a shaft of steel. If the train was fast it might cut many people in two like a knife slicing cucumbers. They shuddered.

A long way beyond the station, there was a dot of light. It went out and another came up nearer. Then another and another, getting nearer and nearer as the train came on. The men looked at the lights and listened to the sound of the train. No one looked at the bridge any more.

A man started climbing on the steel span. He was noticed only when he had got to the top where the rope was tied. They thought he was testing the knot. He was tugging at it. It was well tied; even if the engine funnel hit it, the rope might snap but the knot would not give. The man stretched himself on the rope. His feet were near the knot; his hands almost reached the center of the rope. He was a big man.

The train got closer and closer. The demon form of the engine with sparks flying from its funnel came up along the track. Its puffing was drowned in the roar of the train itself. The whole train could be seen clearly against the wan moonlight. From the coal-tender to the tail end, there was a solid crust of human beings on the roof.

The man was still stretched on the rope.

The leader stood up and shouted hysterically: "Come off, you ass! You will be killed. Come off at once!"

The man turned round toward the voice. He whipped out a small kirpan from his waist and began to slash at the rope.

"Who is this? What is he . . . ?"

There was no time. They looked from the bridge to the train, from the train to the bridge. The man hacked the rope vigorously.

The leader raised his rifle to his shoulder and fired. He hit his mark and one of the man's legs came off the rope and dangled in the air. The other was still twined round the rope. He slashed away in frantic haste. The engine was only a few yards off, throwing embers high up in the sky with each blast of the whistle. Somebody fired another shot. The man's body slid off the rope, but he clung to it with his hands and chin. He pulled himself up, caught the rope under his left armpit, and again started hacking with his right hand. The rope had been cut in shreds. Only a thin tough strand remained. He went at it with the knife, and then with his teeth. The engine was almost on him. There was a volley of shots. The man shivered and collapsed. The rope snapped in the center as he fell. The train went over him, and went on to Pakistan.